*The Masterworks of Literature Series*

WILLIAM S. OSBORNE, *Editor*
*Southern Connecticut State College*

# *Franklin Evans*

# Franklin Evans

or

# The Inebriate

*A Tale of the Times*

by WALTER WHITMAN

*Edited for the Modern Reader by*
Jean Downey
SOUTHERN CONNECTICUT STATE COLLEGE

COLLEGE & UNIVERSITY PRESS • *Publishers*
NEW HAVEN, CONN.

Library of Congress Catalog Card Number: 66-28900



MANUFACTURED IN THE UNITED STATES OF AMERICA BY
UNITED PRINTING SERVICES, INC.
NEW HAVEN, CONN.

# Contents

# Introduction

Of all Whitman's work only a temperance novel, ***Franklin Evans; or The Inebriate, A Tale of the Times,*** was a best-seller. And if what the poet said in his old age is true, then this was the only writing for which he ever received cash in advance and a bonus afterward. His other assertion that he wrote the tract while he sipped intoxicants is not to be taken seriously at all; for when *Franklin Evans* originally appeared in 1842 Whitman was not only abstemious but also sincere in his plea for prohibition, one of the many reforms in which he would maintain an interest for years. There is no uncertainty, however, about that year's being a wonderful, stimulating time for him; he was working as a printer, writer, and editor in Manhattan, "City of hurried and sparkling waters! City of spires and masts! City nested in bays!" And he was twenty-three years of age. Prior to that period his life was apparently so ordinary as to be dull, yet so seemingly prophetic as to warrant recounting.

Walt (whose given name was Walter) Whitman was born on May 31, 1819, at West Hills near Huntington, Long Island, New York, of English, Dutch, and Welsh stock. It is in "There Was a Child Went Forth" that his father, Walter Whitman, a carpenter and builder of "varying fortune," and his mother Louisa Van Velsor Whitman, dearest love of his life, as well as some of "childhood's scenes, absorptions" are reputedly portrayed:

The mother at home quietly placing the dishes on the
    supper-table,
The mother with mild words, clean her cap and gown, a
    wholesome odor falling off her person and clothes as
    she walks by,
The father, strong, self-sufficient, manly, mean, anger'd,
    unjust,

The blow, the quick loud word, the tight bargain, the crafty lure,

The family usages, the language, the company, the furniture, the yearning and swelling heart,

Affection that will not be gainsay'd, the sense of what is real, the thought if after all it should prove unreal,

The doubts of day-time and the doubts of night-time, the curious whether and how,

Whether that which appears so is so, or is it all flashes and specks?

. . . . . . . . . .

The horizon's edge, the flying sea-crow, the fragrance of salt marsh and shore mud,

These became part of that child who went forth every day, and who now goes, and will always go forth every day.

When Whitman was four years old the family moved to Brooklyn, then a sylvan retreat, in the hope of the father's profiting from the building expansion in the bay area of New York. There Walt attended the public schools for approximately six years and St. Ann's Episcopal Sunday school for probably a like period. His parents, however, were not members of a particular church although his mother's mother, to whom Walt was devoted, had been a Quaker; and his father had great admiration for Elias Hicks, the Quaker. "It must have been about 1829 to '30 that I went with my father and mother to hear Elias Hicks preach in a ballroom on Brooklyn Heights," Whitman says in *Specimen Days*.[1] Hicks, who was forced to preach in a hotel because he was barred from churches, had a special place in the poet's affections; indeed,

[1] *The Complete Writings of Walt Whitman*, ed. Richard Maurice Bucke, Thomas B. Harned, and Horace L. Traubel (New York, 1902), IV, 17. Cited hereafter as *CW*.

many of the Quaker allusions interspersed in *Leaves of Grass* may be ascribed to this early influence.

The prosperity and growth that were manifest for Brooklyn did not materialize for Whitman's father who was unfortunate in his real estate speculations. Walt, the second child in the family,[2] went to work therefore when he was about twelve years old. His first employment was as an office boy, at one time for a doctor and at another for lawyers—the Clarkes—at Fulton near Orange Street. Of this situation the poet relates:

> I had a nice desk and window nook to myself; Edward C. kindly helped me at my handwriting and composition, and (the signal event of my life up to that time) subscribed for me to a big circulating library. For a time I now reveled in romance reading of all kinds, first *The Arabian Nights,* all the volumes, an amazing treat. Then, with sorties in very many other directions, took in Walter Scott's novels, one after another, and his poetry (and continue to enjoy novels and poetry to this day).[3]

About two years later he was an apprentice in a weekly newspaper and printing office. The newspaper was the Long Island *Patriot,* Democratic in politics (as were the Whitmans); and its editor, Samuel E. Clements, Quaker and Southerner, was also the owner of the print shop. It was he who gave Whitman one of the keys to life when he allowed the youth to contribute "sentimental bits" to the paper. Another benefactor at the shop was "the veteran printer of the United States" William Hartshorne, a Revolutionary character of whom Walt said: "Hartshorne . . . was a special friend of mine and I had many a talk with him about long-past times."[4] Incidentally, Walt and the other apprentices lived

[2] Of Walt's immediate family, which would eventually include six brothers (one to die in infancy) and two sisters, several were victimized in varying degrees by mental or physical deficiencies.

[3] *CW,* IV, 17-18.

[4] *Ibid.,* p. 18.

with Hartshorne's granddaughter. But learning the printing trade did not take all of his time; and whenever he could, in the evening and on Sundays, he took a ferry ride to New York, there to see the wonderful sights of Manhattan, one day to be called by him "my city!"

The youth next found employment in the office of the Long Island *Star*. That paper was edited by Alden Spooner, well known for his support of civic reforms, health, and temperance movements. And of this period the poet writes:

> I developed (1833-4-5) into a healthy, strong youth (grew too fast, though, was nearly as big as a man at 15 or 16). Our family at this period moved back to the country, my dear mother very ill for a long time, but recovered. All these years I was down Long Island more or less every summer, now east, now west, sometimes months at a stretch. At 16, 17, and so on, was fond of debating societies, and had an active membership with them, off and on, in Brooklyn and one or two country towns on the island. A most omnivorous novel-reader, these and later years, devoured everything I could get. Fond of the theater, also, in New York, went whenever I could—sometimes witnessing fine performances.[5]

His apprenticeship having been completed by 1835, Whitman went to work as a journeyman printer in New York City. But two great fires there that year helped bring on a depression and a halt to his employment in the city.

From about 1836 to 1841 he taught in country schools in Queens and Suffolk counties, Long Island, his qualifications for teaching deriving from the skills and knowledge gained in the printing business. In his comments on the poet's life for this time Canby notes:

> Thoreau, in the same years, with a Harvard degree, was beginning in the public school of Concord. He did not need his B.A. degree for the job. Teaching was the

[5] *Ibid.*, p. 19.

> obvious thing for youngsters professionally inclined, who needed some means of subsistence while they got under way. The surprising parallel between the two youths is the similarity and (for that day) originality of their methods. Thoreau would not strap his pupils, and so lost his first position. Whitman, under no influence of which we are aware, also managed his classes without physical punishment, read poetry to them instead of sermonizing, and, in that easy-going community, seems not to have been rebuked. Henry and John Thoreau, likewise, when they opened their academy, substituted interesting talks on nature and science for the moral lecturing regarded as indispensable. Deep influences of a new individualism, far deeper than personal taste, were at work upon these pioneers of the nineteenth century.[6]

In those days a country schoolteacher's salary for a three months' term was approximately $40, with the teacher living under the "boarded round" system: staying for a few days at a time with the families of his students. Whitman considered this "one of my best experiences and deepest lessons in human nature behind the scenes and in the masses."[7]

Having time enough now, Whitman in 1838 began his own weekly newspaper, the *Long Islander;* and this is his remembered account:

> I went to New York, bought a press and types, hired some little help, but did most of the work myself, including the press-work. Everything seem'd turning out well (only my own restlessness prevented me gradually establishing a permanent property there). I bought a good horse, and every week went all round the country serving my papers, devoting one day and night to it. I never had happier jaunts—going over to south side, to Babylon, down the south road, across to Smithtown and

[6] Henry Seidel Canby, *Walt Whitman, an American* (Boston, 1943), pp. 24-25.

[7] *CW*, IV, 20.

> Comac, and back home. The experiences of those jaunts, the dear old-fashion'd farmers and their wives, the stops by the hayfields, the hospitality, nice dinners, occasional evenings, the girls, the rides through the brush, come up in my memory to this day.[8]

Within a year's time Whitman was teaching again, in a school near Jamaica, and in his out of school hours was typesetting for the Long Island *Democrat;* to this weekly newspaper he contributed some of his early verse and a series of articles called the "Sun-Down Papers from the Desk of a School-Master." In one of these he tells of several kinds of intemperance:

> Amidst the universal excitement which appears to have been created of late years, with regard to the evils created by ardent spirits, it seems to have been forgotten that there are other, and almost as injurious, kinds of intemperance. The practice of using tobacco, in any shape, is one of these. . . . The excessive use of tea and coffee, too, is a species of intemperance much to be condemned. . . . Into what ridiculous lengths can people be led by fashion! Hot drinks of this kind are fatal to the teeth, deleterious to physical strength, the cause of impure blood, and the means of producing many a head ache, many a pale face, and many an emaciated body.[9]

Whitman was apparently not too concerned, however, with the injurious effect of coffee and other drinks when he was in New Orleans in 1848:

> One of my choice amusements during my stay in New Orleans was going down to the old French Market, especially of a Sunday morning. The show was a varied and curious one; among the rest, the Indian and negro

[8] *CW*, V, 34.

[9] *The Uncollected Poetry and Prose of Walt Whitman: Much of Which Has Been But Recently Discovered with Various Early Manuscripts Now First Published,* ed. Emory Holloway (New York, 1932), I, 32-33. Cited hereafter as *UPP.*

hucksters with their wares. For there were always fine specimens of Indians, both men and women, young and old. I remember I nearly always on these occasions got a large cup of delicious coffee with a biscuit, for my breakfast, from the immense shining copper kettle of a great Creole mulatto woman (I believe she weigh'd 230 pounds). I never have had such coffee since. About nice drinks, anyhow, my recollection of the "cobblers" (with strawberries and snow on top of the large tumblers), and also the exquisite wines, and the perfect and mild French brandy, help the regretful reminiscence of my New Orleans experience of those days.[10]

But in Whitman's particular world of 1840 much more was happening. He was twenty-one years of age, active in politics (campaigning that fall in Queens County for the reelection of President Van Buren) and concerned about his capacity for doing great things. He asks in one of his "Sun-Down Papers": "Who should be a better judge of a man's talents than the man himself? I see no reason why we should let our lights shine under bushels. Yes: I *would* write a book! And who shall say that it might not be a very pretty book? Who knows but that I might do something very respectable?"[11] In a vaguely ambitious way, then, Whitman turned away from teaching in the spring of 1841 to take up his interest full time in the printing trade in New York City where the expansion of the daily press and literary periodicals was unparalleled. He went to work as a compositor in the office of the *New World* (the first number of the weekly had been issued June 6, 1840). It was one of the mammoth weeklies given to serial fiction, some of which had been borrowed from other sources, usually English authors.

Its pages were sometimes more than four feet long and eleven columns wide: Griswold [the Rev. Rufus Wilmot Griswold, later to be the literary executor of Poe] was

[10] *CW*, VI, 210.
[11] *UPP*, I, 37.

wont to call such issues "Leviathan" sheets, with a capital L. After six months the *New World* began to publish a quarto edition as well as the monster folio, and it was eventually followed in this by the *Brother Jonathan.* But serial publication of popular English writers like Dickens and Bulwer was too slow: the pirating book-publishers would seize upon a volume as soon as it was received from England, and rush it into print before the periodicals had a chance at it. The Harper brothers would have their meals brought to them in their shop, and even sleep on the floor of the composing-room, in order to hasten the issue of such a work and be first in the bookshops with it. So the *New World* and *Brother Jonathan* set out to beat the book publishers at their own game, and to issue complete novels as "extras." They would have their messengers awaiting the steamships to board them before they docked, and receive the earliest copies of the new English novels; they would then rush the books into type by working large forces of typesetters night and day, and within twenty-four hours would have them on the streets, damp from the presses, being cried by the newsboys: "Extry! Dickens' new novel! Only ten cents a copy!" And the purchaser of a G. P. R. James or Dickens novel in eighty closely-printed quarto pages would forget the injury to his eyes in the savings to his pocketbook. Benjamin [Park Benjamin, editor and publisher of the *New World,* was among those successfully sued for libel by J. F. Cooper] was in his glory: he taunted the piratical book publishers, and he talked playfully to his readers. "You are not so green as to give a dollar for what you can get for eighteen pence or a shilling—not you!" he wrote in the *New World.*[12]

Whitman's life was made more eventful that year not only because he was a typesetter for the *New World* but also because he began his contributions to one of the leading American periodicals of the day, the *Democratic Review.* In its

[12] Frank Luther Mott, *A History of American Magazines, 1741-1850* (Cambridge, Massachusetts, 1957), I, 359-60.

pages appeared the work of Bryant, Lowell, Whittier, Hawthorne, and Poe. The August, 1841, issue carried the first of Whitman's stories, "Death in the Schoolroom"—a tale of Lugare, a cruel schoolmaster, and Tim Barker, a good natured, frail schoolboy. After being wrongfully reproached by the schoolmaster, the terrified boy falls asleep in class. The teacher enraged by the boy's indifference to his repeated taunts begins beating him about the back and shoulders. "But still Tim show'd no signs of motion; and as Lugare, provoked at his torpidity, jerk'd away one of the child's arms . . . his head dropp'd down on the board with a dull sound. . . ." Characteristically, the moral of the story is in the last sentence: "Death was in the schoolroom, and Lugare had been flogging a CORPSE."[13]

Short fiction was part of the popular fare in American periodicals in the second quarter of the nineteenth century, and it had been notably advanced by Edgar Allan Poe, who was ten years older than Whitman. Poe had turned from poetry to fiction when he was in his early twenties; in fact, at twenty-four he had won with "MS. Found in a Bottle" a prize of fifty dollars offered for the best story by the Baltimore *Saturday Visiter*. For the rest of his life Poe would continue with the short story, but not, however, abandoning his interest in poetry. Some of the best known of his verse would appear in his last years, but the bulk of it was published before he was twenty-two. With Whitman just the opposite was true, for all his fiction was published when he was in his twenties; after that, his main interest would be poetry.

Poe's short stories are world famous; Whitman's are in the dustbins of literature. And that is where the poet himself would have them, except at that time they did add to his importance as a member of the press. After he left the *New World* (in which, incidentally, was published some of his verse as well as his fiction), he went to work as an editor

[13] *CW*, VI, 14-15.

sometime in February, 1842, for the *Aurora* and later that same year for the *Evening Tattler*. In those days of the quick rise and fall of newspapers and magazines, a frequent change of jobs was not unusual. Additionally, it was a time when the newspaper was the expression of a dominant personality; and the youthful Whitman described then as usually wearing a frock coat and high hat, carrying a small cane, and ornamenting the lapel of his coat with a boutonniere, undoubtedly believed that he could add his name to the list of notable journalists of the day. As editor of the *Aurora* he involved himself in political controversies, interested his readers in reforms, and assailed other editors including Park Benjamin, his former employer on the *New World*. Benjamin seemed not to mind the attack too much; he apparently considered it part of the game. Besides, as one of the editors interested in sensational journalistic devices and huge sales, Benjamin could use Whitman's reputation as a newspaperman and his prestige as a steady contributor of fiction to the *Democratic Review* in the exploitation of temperance tracts.

One of the countless reforms that arose in America in the nineteenth century was the temperance movement. It had its beginnings in 1808 at Saratoga Springs, New York; and there in 1836 at the second annual convention, members of the American Temperance Union advocated, as one of the most valuable persuaders to the cause, fiction—narratives of those who were regenerated by the pledge. So eagerly were these stories sought by publishers and readers alike that prepublication notices were usually part of the appeal. The announcement of *Franklin Evans* reads:

FRIENDS OF TEMPERANCE, AHOY!

Franklin Evans,

or

The Inebriate

A Tale of the Times.—By a Popular American Author.

THIS NOVEL, which is dedicated to the Temperance Societies and the friends of the Temperance Cause throughout the Union, will create a sensation, both for the ability with which it is written, as well as the interest of the subject, and will be universally read and admired. It was written expressly for the NEW WORLD, by one of the best Novelists of this country, with a view to aid the great work of Reform, and rescue Young Men from the demon of Intemperance. The incidents of the plot are wrought out with great effect, and the excellence of its moral, and the beneficial influence it will have, should interest the friends of Temperance Reformation in giving this Tale the widest possible circulation.

Terms.—It will be issued in an Extra *New World*, (octavo,) on Wednesday, Nov. 23, at 12½ cents single; ten copies for $1, or $8 pr hundred. Let the orders be early.

Address, postpaid, J. Winchester, 30 Ann St. N.Y.[14]

When it appeared in the *New World, Franklin Evans* was made up of an INTRODUCTORY and twenty-five chapters, each of which had a motto,[15] except the last which bore the word CONCLUSION. And the identity of the "Popular American Author" was now revealed; under the tale's title appeared "By Walter Whitman."

In his introductory remarks Whitman tells the reader that *Franklin Evans* is a plain story of a country youth who went to the city to seek his fortune but who was "thrown by circumstances amid the vortex of dissipation." He then goes on to hope the story will do good: "Issued in the cheap and popular form you see, and wafted by every mail to all parts of this vast republic . . . its being written *for the mass* . . . the fact that it is as a pioneer in this department of literature

[14] *UPP*, II, 103-4.

[15] Both Thomas Ollive Mabbott and Emory Holloway have identified the sources of the mottoes in *Franklin Evans*. See Holloway's *UPP*, II, and Mabbott "Notes on Walt Whitman's *'Franklin Evans,'*" *Notes and Queries*, CLXXXIX (December, 1925), 419-20.

—all these will give 'The Inebriate,' I feel confident, a more than ordinary share of patronage." Finally, aware of the "faults and deficiencies" of the work, the writer says: "Yet my book is not written for the critics, but for THE PEOPLE."[16] The people certainly did not mind the shortcomings of these tracts as works of art, for "Over 12 per cent of the novels published in America during the 1830's dealt with temperance, and though they were mostly brief tracts disguised as fiction and distributed free, they had a great circulation. Even as late as the Civil War years, the American Temperance Union shipped two million pieces of propaganda (much of it fiction) to the army and navy, where soldiers and sailors probably read it in lieu of anything better."[17] Gruesomeness, tragedy, and corpses (preferably bloated) were a few of the ingredients of most of the tracts. And in *Franklin Evans,* "a thrilling romance," Whitman served up a dish of popular taste.

*Franklin Evans* is a long-winded account of a Long Island youth who goes to Manhattan, takes to drink, and sinks by stages to the lowest of occupations, barkeeping. He marries and reforms but soon returns to his old habit. His wife dies (from heartbreak) and he falls in with a gang. He is jailed but quickly rescued and rehabilitated by one who understands the problem of intemperance. He then signs the Old Pledge, "which forbade only the drinking of the most ardent kind of liquors, and allowed people to get as much fuddled as they chose upon wines, and beer, and so on."[18] He travels to

[16] Walter Whitman, *Franklin Evans; or The Inebriate. A Tale of the Times,* with an Introduction by Jean Downey (New Haven, 1966), pp. 35-36.

One of the most popular of temperance novelists was Lucius Manlius Sargent. "His first tale, *My Mother's Gold Ring,* was issued in 1833; within six years its title page proclaimed '113th thousand.'" See James D. Hart, *The Popular Book; A History of America's Literary Taste* (Berkeley, California, 1961), p. 109, for other early temperance novelists. Thus, Whitman's *Franklin Evans* was not, as he writes, "a pioneer in this department of literature."

[17] Hart, p. 108.

[18] *Franklin Evans,* p. 136.

Virginia where his mind becomes *"obfusticated"* by the drinking of wine. There he marries a beautiful Creole girl and almost immediately becomes involved with a white woman who drives the Creole to madness, murder, and suicide. He returns to New York City; this time his reform is complete, for he signs the bond of "total abstinence." In his closing remarks Whitman hopes his narrative has amused and edified the reader, pays honor to the Washingtonians,[19] warns young men away from "musical drinking-shops . . . where the mind and the body are both rendered effeminate together," and says that if his story meets with favor readers might hear from him again.[20]

## II

The earliest recorded criticism of *Franklin Evans* is that made by Whitman himself. On May 2, 1888, the poet said:

> "I doubt if there is a copy in existence. I have none and have not had one for years; it was a pamphlet. Parke Godwin and another somebody (who was it?) came to see me about writing it. Their offer of cash payment was so tempting—I was hard up at the time—that I set to work at once ardently on it (with the help of a bottle of port or what not). In three days of constant work I finished the book. Finished the book? Finished myself. It was damned rot—rot of the worst sort—not insincere perhaps, but rot, nevertheless: it was not the business for me to be up to. I stopped right there: I never cut a chip off that kind of timber again."[21]

[19] The Washington Temperance Society was formed in Baltimore in 1840; its founders were "six convivial friends–artisans by day, tipplers and gamesters by night. . . ."

[20] In his book, *Free and Lonesome Heart: The Secret of Walt Whitman,* Holloway writes: "Though I have found only a fragment preserved in an old temperance newspaper, within three months of the publication of *Franklin Evans,* he did at least begin the serialization of a novel called *The Madman.* Like *Franklin Evans* it was propaganda for the temperance cause, the scene is laid in New York and the first-person character is a young man bearing a resemblance to Whitman himself."

[21] Horace L. Traubel, *With Walt Whitman in Camden* (Boston, 1906), I, 93.

Four months later—in September, 1888—*Franklin Evans* was mentioned again by the poet in a conversation he had with his friends Horace Traubel and Thomas Harned about two bottles of wine. Whitman said:

> "Let's open one—shall we? Will you take a glass?" Took up the bottle. "You won't do like a fellow I had here a little while ago: he sat across from me, as you do—saw me open the bottle for him—then said he was a temperance man, or something—never drank at all." W. took a cork-screw out of his pocket and handed it with the bottle to me. "Open it, Horace." I laughed. "Do you carry the cork-screw about with you, Walt?" "Yes." Harned said: "That's bad, Walt—they'll throw you out of the temperance society." "They can't—I never was in." I asked: "But didn't you write a temperance novel once?" "Yes, so I did—for seventy-five dollars cash down. And, by the way, that seventy-five dollars was not the end of it, for the book sold so well they sent me fifty dollars more in two or three weeks."[22]

Whitman's comments about his temperance novel were usually good-humored. He differed from Hawthorne, for example, who when questioned about an early work of his titled *Fanshawe,* published anonymously in 1828 (Hawthorne was then twenty-four), answered his publisher James T. Fields as follows:

> "You make an inquiry about some supposed former publication of mine. I cannot be sworn to make correct answers as to all the literary or other follies of my nonage; and I earnestly recommend you not to brush away the dust that may have gathered over them. Whatever might do me credit you may be pretty sure I should be ready enough to bring forward. Anything else it is our mutual interest to conceal; and so far from assisting your re-

[22] *Ibid.,* II, 322-23.

searches in that direction, I especially enjoin it on you, my dear friend, not to read any unacknowledged page that you may suppose to be mine."[23]

But Whitman persisted in droll explanations of how his novel came to be written. "He wrote it," says a lifelong acquaintance, "mostly in the reading room of Tammany Hall, which was a sort of Bohemian resort, and he afterward told me that he frequently indulged in gin cocktails while writing it, at the 'Pewter Mug,' another resort for Bohemians around the corner in Spruce Street."[24]

Of course, many of Whitman's critics have not taken *Franklin Evans* seriously. One of his early biographers who did not doubt the poet's sincerity as an advocate of temperance did, however, confidently predict that the tale would never be reprinted.[25] Another believed that the inset stories in Chapter II (The Indian tale), Chapter XIV (the story of Little Jane), and Chapter XXI (the dream) could be omitted entirely. Holloway judges that "they were inserted either because Whitman had them already on hand and did not scruple to reuse them as padding (for subsequently he did reprint two of them as new tales), or else because he thought they would vary somewhat the interest of an otherwise monotonous relation. The Indian legend, for instance, might be expected to please a public which was clamoring for native themes in the annuals and magazines no less than in Cooper's novels."[26] Allen agrees that the imbedded stories were used to pad the manuscript, asserting they are evidence of the haste with which *Franklin Evans* was written. And Cowie thinks that "the structure of the book . . . is rendered the more defective"

[23] James T. Fields, *Yesterdays with Authors* (Boston, 1925), p. 48.
[24] Bliss Perry, *Walt Whitman* (London, 1906), p. 28.
[25] Henry Bryan Binns, *A Life of Walt Whitman* (New York, 1905), p. 36.
[26] *Franklin Evans* . . . with an Introduction by Emory Holloway (New York, 1929), p. xiii.

by these stories.[27] In commenting upon another aspect, this same critic writes that when the story moves to Virginia, Whitman "missed a chance to speak eloquently on slavery, a topic which the Mexican War would soon bring sharply into focus."[28]

His treatment of slavery also caused Newton Arvin to say that "Whitman had apologized, with evident discomfort, for the peculiar institution of the South. There is a character in that little tract, a French émigré, who in spite of the most advanced political sentiments has become a plantation-owner and slave-holder in Virginia, and who compares in his own mind the tangible miseries of the European proletariat with the 'merely nominal oppression' of the American Negroes!"[29] And another biographer says: "But when the tale goes to the South (of which Walt then knew nothing), 'melodramatic' is too weak a word to describe its incidents and characters, 'sentimental' too mild to define its morality, and 'tripe' too gentle a name for its eloquence." Frances Winwar would wonder, however, if there were not something more to this part of the story.

> Had Walt seen Margaret's counterpart in one of the "musical drinking-houses" which he depicted in such detail in his novel, or had she been one of the countless women whose beauty he had surreptitiously admired in the streets of New York? In spite of the diffidence that made Walt, the author, underline how near white her complexion really was, he dwelt too lovingly upon Margaret's charms for the description to be wholly objective. Had he like Franklin Evans been attracted by one of her dusky sisters and, more successfully than his hero, had he resisted temptation with the illiberal argument, "But she was not of my race. . . . What had I to do with such as she?" His words were not without signifi-

[27] Alexander Cowie, *The Rise of the American Novel* (New York, 1948), p. 308.
[28] *Ibid.*
[29] Newton Arvin, *Whitman* (New York, 1938), p. 35.

> cance, at least in their indication of what type of woman could stir his emotions. If he had succumbed to any such charmer of flesh and blood he kept the knowledge from everyone.[30]

Women and Whitman, particularly in the 1840's, provide an autobiographical clue for another critic who states: "Only two years before writing 'Franklin Evans' Whitman had declared in print that neither by experience nor by observation had he learned anything about women; yet in this dream-like story the future author of 'Children of Adam' passes through a varied experience with the sex: a back-stage disillusionment, an unreal marriage, an illicit flirtation, an idealization of the wife and mother, and even a drink-inspired entanglement with an octoroon, whose chief recommendation is her voluptuous appeal to his senses. And as to this last, there are those who will see in it a strange adumbration of what happened to Whitman in New Orleans less than six years later."[31] Leslie Fiedler, in commenting upon the different uses American writers made of dark and fair ladies, includes Whitman: "In other writers, the symbolic contrast recurs as a cliché or a scarcely noticed convention: the blond, scatter-brained Rowena and the tragic mulatto Roxana in *Pudd'nhead Wilson;* or the seduced and avenging Laura Van Brunt and the Quaker Nice Girl, Ruth Bolton, in Twain's one 'serious' novel *The Gilded Age;* or the death-ridden Creole Margaret and Mrs. Conway with 'her light hair, blue eyes, and delicacy . . . of skin' who intrude so inappropriately upon Whitman's temperance novel, *Franklin Evans.*"[32]

The city and the youthful Whitman's reaction to it do not at all surprise Fiedler. "It is, indeed, quite what one would expect from the perpetual mama's boy, as obsessed as Dreiser

[30] Frances Winwar, *American Giant: Walt Whitman and His Times* (New York, 1941), p. 79.
[31] Holloway, Introduction to *Franklin Evans,* p. xvi.
[32] Leslie Fiedler, *Love and Death in the American Novel* (Cleveland, 1962), p. 286.

by the image of the enduring mother, and the refugee from a small town, breathless before the big city with its infinite possibilities of sin. 'City of Orgies,' Whitman was to call New York in a much later poem, and city of orgies it is in his first and only novel."[33] Van Wyck Brooks too considered the tale to be one of many warnings against the dangers of the city "at a time when modern urban life was just beginning in the United States and all the towns were full of young men from the country."[34] And Canby adds: "There are good scenes . . . fresh from Whitman's memory, of his apprentice days in New York, descriptions of the 'musical drinking-houses,' the streets, the shops, the typical characters encountered by a young fellow trying to get started in a great city."[35] Charles Dickens visited New York early in the year that *Franklin Evans* was published and observed that "The beautiful metropolis of America is by no means so clean a city as Boston. . . ."[36] As to the amusements on and about the lower Broadway area where he walked and where Whitman at the time lived and worked,[37] the English novelist writes:

> Are there no amusements? Yes, there is a lecture-room across the way, from which that glare of light proceeds, and there may be evening service for the ladies thrice a week, or oftener. For the young gentlemen there is the counting-house, the store, the bar-room; the latter, as you may see through these windows, pretty full. Hark! to the clinking sound of hammers breaking lumps of ice,

[33] *Ibid.*, p. 260.

[34] Van Wyck Brooks, *The Times of Melville and Whitman* (New York, 1953), p. 143.

[35] Canby, p. 41.

[36] Charles Dickens, *American Notes* (Greenwich, Connecticut, 1961), p. 99.

[37] In a manuscript notebook Whitman wrote the following entries: "Went to New York in May 1841 and wrote for *Democratic Review*, worked at printing business in *New World* office; boarded at Mrs. Chipmans—Went in April 1842 to edit *Aurora* . . . Fall and winter of 1842 boarded at Mrs. R. in Spring st. . . . Edited *Tattler* in summer of '42." See *UPP*, II, 87-88.

> and to the cool gurgling of the pounded bits, as, in the process of mixing, they are poured from glass to glass! No amusements? What are these suckers of cigars and swallowers of strong drinks, whose hats and legs we see in every possible variety of twist, doing, but amusing themselves? What are the fifty newspapers, which those precocious urchins are bawling down the street, and which are kept filed within, what are they but amusements? Not vapid, waterish amusements, but good strong stuff; dealing in round abuse and blackguard names; pulling off the roofs of private houses, as the Halting Devil did in Spain; pimping and pandering for all degrees of vicious taste, and gorging with coined lies the most voracious maw; imputing to every man in public life the coarsest and the vilest motives; scaring away from the stabbed and prostrate body politic every Samaritan of clear conscience and good deeds; and setting on, with yell and whistle, and the clapping of foul hands, the vilest vermin and worst birds of prey.—No amusements![38]

Years later, in his own recollection of the Broadway area, Whitman said:

> And who remembers the renown'd New York "Tabernacle" of those days "before the war"? It was on the east side of Broadway, near Pearl Street—was a great turtle-shaped hall, and you had to walk back from the street entrance thro' a long wide corridor to get to it—was very strong—had an immense gallery—altogether held three or four thousand people. Here the huge annual conventions of the windy and cyclonic "reformatory societies" of those times were held—especially the tumultuous Anti-Slavery ones. I remember hearing Wendell Phillips, Emerson, Cassius Clay, John P. Hale, Beecher, Fred Douglas [sic], the Burleighs, Garrison and others. Sometimes the Hutchinsons would sing—very fine. Sometimes there were angry rows. A chap named Isaiah Rhynders, a fierce politician of those days, with a band of robust supporters, would attempt to

[38] Dickens, pp. 107-8.

contradict the speakers and break up the meetings. But the Anti-Slavery, and Quaker, and Temperance, and Missionary and conventicles and speakers were tough, tough, and always maintained their ground, and carried out their programs fully. I went frequently to these meetings, May after May—learn'd much from them—was sure to be on hand when J. P. Hale or Cash Clay made speeches. There were also the smaller and handsome halls of the Historical and Athenaeum Societies up on Broadway. I very well remember W. C. Bryant lecturing on Homoeopathy in one of them, and attending two or three addressed by R. W. Emerson in the other.[39]

Whitman had other favorities, and Dickens was one of them. In fact, in that very same year (1842) that the English novelist commented on the "amusements" in the Broadway area, Whitman wrote an article "Boz and Democracy." Dickens had been attacked by the editor of the Washington *Globe* for delineating the human character in its lowest stage of ignorance, vice, and degradation and for giving it the most unbounded scope in every species of wickedness and crime.[40] Whitman considered Dickens to be a democratic writer. "He not only teaches his readers to abhor vice," Whitman wrote, "but he exhibits before them, for imitation, examples of the beauty of honesty—not as in the abstract style of the essayist, or the lofty dreams of the poet—but by examples that everyone can copy, examples in familiar life, that come home to us all."[41]

Dickens's influence upon Whitman and especially in *Franklin Evans* is dimly seen by several biographers but is particularly evident for one who writes: "In the narrative the Dickensian play of contrasts works overtime: the rich criminal gorges at the banquet; the hapless stealer of a loaf dies at hard labor. Innocent childhood begs for its drunken parent;

[39] *CW*, VII, 54-55.
[40] *UPP*, I, 67.
[41] *Ibid.*, pp. 69-70.

guilty experience inducts simplicity to its own evil practices. No doubt Walt believed he was writing a social document. He relied too much, however, upon his notion of what constituted social realities and too little on experience. But then, as he declared, he was not writing for critics."[42]

Some modern readers will undoubtedly agree with critics who have said that *Franklin Evans* is "an atrocious novel," "an outrageous piece of vulgarity," "nothing but an intellectual caprice"; that it "showed the effect of confused mentality, due to some cause or other, in its cheap style and manner of narrative"; and that it is a "thoroughly worthless production for a man at any age, and Whitman had come to twenty-three years." Other modern readers will join those who have seen some merit in its autobiographical significance, in its "sympathy with the poor and the suffering," and in its value as an early temperance tract. A few readers may enjoy it for itself.

JEAN DOWNEY

*New Haven, Connecticut*

[42] Winwar, p. 76.

## Selected Bibliography

ALLEN, GAY WILSON. *The Solitary Singer: A Critical Biography of Walt Whitman.* New York: Grove Press, 1955.

ARVIN, NEWTON. *Whitman.* New York: The Macmillan Company, 1938.

BINNS, HENRY BRYAN. *A Life of Walt Whitman.* New York: E. P. Dutton and Company, 1905.

BROOKS, VAN WYCK. *The Times of Melville and Whitman.* New York: E. P. Dutton and Company, 1953.

CANBY, HENRY SEIDEL. *Walt Whitman, an American.* Boston: Houghton Mifflin Company, 1943.

*The Complete Writings of Walt Whitman,* ed. RICHARD MAURICE BUCKE, THOMAS B. HARNED, HORACE L. TRAUBEL. 10 vols. New York: G. P. Putnam's Sons, 1902.

COWIE, ALEXANDER. *The Rise of the American Novel.* New York: American Book Company, 1948.

DICKENS, CHARLES. *American Notes.* Greenwich, Connecticut: Fawcett Publications, 1961.

FIEDLER, LESLIE. *Love and Death in the American Novel.* Cleveland: World Publishing Company, 1962.

FIELDS, JAMES T. *Yesterdays with Authors.* Boston: Houghton Mifflin Company, 1925.

HART, JAMES D. *The Popular Book; A History of America's Literary Taste.* Berkeley, California: University of California Press, 1961.

HOLLOWAY, EMORY. *Free and Lonesome Heart: The Secret of Walt Whitman.* New York: Vantage Press, 1960.

MABBOTT, THOMAS OLLIVE. "Notes on Walt Whitman's 'Franklin Evans,'" *Notes and Queries,* CLXXXIX (December, 1925), 419-20.

MOTT, FRANK LUTHER. *A History of American Magazines.* 4 vols. Cambridge, Massachusetts: Harvard University Press, 1957.

PERRY, BLISS. *Walt Whitman.* London: Archibald Constable & Co., Ltd., 1906.

TRAUBEL, HORACE L. *With Walt Whitman in Camden.* Vol. I, Boston: Small Maynard and Company, 1906. Vol. II, New York: D. Appleton and Company, 1908. Vol. III, New York: Mitchell Kennerly, 1914.

*The Uncollected Poetry and Prose of Walt Whitman,* collected and edited by EMORY HOLLOWAY. 2 vols. New York: Peter Smith, 1932.

WHITMAN, WALT. *The Early Poems and The Fiction,* ed. THOMAS L. BRASHER. New York: New York University Press, 1963.

———. *Franklin Evans; or The Inebriate, A Tale of the Times.* With an Introduction by EMORY HOLLOWAY. New York: Random House, 1929.

WINWAR, FRANCES. *American Giant: Walt Whitman and His Times.* New York: Harper and Brothers, 1941.

## Notes on the Text

*Franklin Evans; or the Inebriate, A Tale of the Times* was first published in the *New World* II (No. 10, Extra Series No. 34, November, 1842), 1-31. The present text follows a 1929 printing, with capitalization, punctuation, and spelling preserved because they are characteristic of Whitman.

The first issue of the tale apparently sold so well (reportedly 20,000 copies) that it was advertised again in the *New World* on August 19, 1843, but with a slightly changed title: *Franklin Evans; or the Merchant's Clerk: A Tale of the Times.* Republished in the Brooklyn *Daily Eagle,* November 16-30, 1846, while Whitman was editor of the paper, the novel did not include the Introductory, the Conclusion (Chapter XXV), the inset stories, and several incidents. Also, the last part of it was considerably changed; the title had no mention of Franklin Evans; and the author withheld his name and disguised himself as "J. R. S." The heading read: "*A Tale of Long-Island. FORTUNES OF A COUNTRY-BOY; Incidents in Town—and his Adventure at the South.* By J. R. S."

Copies of the first edition were reproduced in 1921 in *The Uncollected Poetry and Prose of Walt Whitman,* collected and edited by Emory Holloway; in 1929 in *Franklin Evans; or the Inebriate, A Tale of the Times,* with an introduction by Emory Holloway; and in 1963 in *The Early Poems and the Fiction,* edited by Thomas L. Brasher.

J. D.

# *Franklin Evans*

# Introductory

THE story I am going to tell you, reader, will be somewhat aside from the ordinary track of the novelist. It will not abound, either with profound reflections, or sentimental remarks. Yet its moral—for I flatter myself it has one, and one which it were well to engrave on the heart of each person who scans its pages—will be taught by its own incidents, and the current of the narrative.

Whatever of romance there may be—I leave it to any who have, in the course of their every-day walks, heard the histories of intemperate men, whether the events of the tale, strange as some of them may appear, have not had their counterpart in real life. If you who live in the city should go out among your neighbors and investigate what is being transacted there, you might come to behold things far more improbable. In fact, the following chapters contain but the account of a young man, thrown by circumstances amid the vortex of dissipation—a country youth, who came to our great emporium to seek his fortune—and what befell him there. So it is a plain story; yet as the grandest truths are sometimes plain enough to enter into the minds of children—it may be that the delineation I shall give will do benefit, and that educated men and women may not find the hour they spend in its perusal altogether wasted.

And I would ask your belief when I assert that what you are going to read is not a work of fiction, as the term is used. I narrate occurrences that have had a far more substantial existence, than in my fancy. There will be those who, as their eyes turn past line after line, will have their memories carried to matters which they have heard of before, or taken a part in themselves, and which, they know, are *real.*

Can I hope, that my story will do good? I entertain that hope. Issued in the cheap and popular form you see, and wafted by every mail to all parts of this vast republic; the facilities which its publisher possesses, giving him the power of diffusing it more widely than any other establishment in the United States; the mighty and deep public opinion which, as a tide bears a ship upon its bosom, ever welcomes anything favorable to the Temperance Reform; its being written *for the mass,* though the writer hopes, not without some claim upon the approval of the more fastidious; and, as much as anything else, the fact that it is as a pioneer in this department of literature—all these will give "The Inebriate," I feel confident, a more than ordinary share of patronage.

For youth, what can be more invaluable? It teaches sobriety, that virtue which every mother and father prays nightly may be resident in the characters of their sons. It wars against Intemperance, that evil spirit which has levelled so many fair human forms before its horrible advances. Without being presumptuous, I would remind those who believe in the wholesome doctrines of abstinence, how the earlier teachers of piety used parables and fables, as the fit instruments whereby they might convey to men the beauty of the system they professed. In the resemblance, how reasonable it is to suppose that you can impress a lesson upon him whom you would influence to sobriety, in no better way than letting him read such a story as this.

It is usual for writers, upon presenting their works to the public, to bespeak indulgence for faults and deficiencies. I am but too well aware that the critical eye will see some such in the following pages; yet my book is not written for the critics, but for *THE PEOPLE;* and while I think it best to leave it to the reader's own decision whether I have succeeded, I cannot help remarking, that I have the fullest confidence in the verdict's being favorable.

And, to conclude, may I hope that he who purchases this volume will give to its author, and to its publisher also, the credit of being influenced not altogether by views of the profit to come from it? Whatever of those views may enter into our minds, we are not without a strong desire that the principles here inculcated will strike deep, and grow again, and bring forth good fruit. A prudent, sober, and temperate course of life cannot be too strongly taught to old and young; to the young, because the future years are before them—to the old, because it is their business to prepare for death. And though, as before remarked, the writer has abstained from thrusting the moral upon the reader, by dry and abstract disquisitions—preferring the more pleasant and quite as profitable method of letting the reader draw it himself from the occurrences—it is hoped that the New and Popular Reform now in the course of progress over the land, will find no trifling help from a TALE OF THE TIMES.

# I

The tree-tops now are glittering in the sun;
Away! 'tis time my journey was begun.

R. H. DANA

ONE bright cool morning in the autumn of 183–, a country market-wagon, which also performed the office of stage-coach for those whose means or dispositions were humble enough to be satisfied with its rude accommodations, was standing, with the horses harnessed before it, in front of a village inn, on the Long Island turnpike. As the geography of the reader may be at fault to tell the exact whereabouts of this locality, I may as well say, that Long Island is a part of the State of New York, and stretches out into the Atlantic, just south-eastward of the city which is the great emporium of our western world. The most eastern county of the island has many pretty towns and hamlets; the soil is fertile, and the people, though not refined or versed in city life, are very intelligent and hospitable. It was in that eastern county, on the side nearest the sea, that the road ran on which the market-wagon just mentioned was going to traverse. The driver was in the bar-room, taking a glass of liquor.

As the landlord, a sickly-looking, red-nosed man, was just counting out the change for the one dollar bill out of which the price of the brandy was to be taken, a stranger entered upon the scene. He was a robust youth, of about twenty years; and he carried an old black leather valise in his hand, and a coarse overcoat hanging on his arm. The proprietor of the vehicle standing outside, knew, with the tact of his trade, the moment this young man hove in sight, that he probably wished to take passage with him. The stranger walked along the narrow path that bordered the road, with a light and springy step; and as he came toward the tavern, the personages who noticed him, thought they saw him brushing something from his eyes—the traces of tears, as it were. Upon the valise which he carried in his hand was tacked a small card, on which was written, *"Franklin Evans."*

Reader, I was that youth; and the words just quoted, are the name of the hero of the tale you have now begun to peruse. Flattered shall I feel, if it be interesting enough to lead you on to the conclusion!

"What, Frank, is it you?" said the landlord's wife to me, coming in from an adjoining room at this moment. "Surely you cannot be going from the village? How are all your uncle's folks this morning? Baggage with you, too! Then it must be that you leave us, indeed."

"I am bound for New York," was my brief answer to the somewhat garrulous dame, as I opened the old-fashioned half-door, and entered the house. I threw my valise upon a bench, and my overcoat upon it.

The good landlady's further inquisitiveness was cut short, by my taking the driver out to his wagon, for the purpose of making arrangements and settling the price of my passage. This was soon concluded, and my rather limited stock of travelling gear was safely deposited on the top of some baskets of mutton in the rear of the vehicle.

"Come, youngster," said he who owned the mutton; "come in with me, and take a drop before we start. The weather is chill, and we need somewhat to keep us warm."

I felt no particular wish either to drink or refuse; so I walked in, and each of us drank off a portion of that fluid, which has brought more wo into society than all the other causes of evil combined, together.

The landlord and his family were old acquaintances of mine, from the fact that we had for several years resided in the same village. It was not, therefore, without some little feeling of displeasure with myself, that I repulsed all the good-natured inquiries and endeavors of him and his wife, to discover the object of my journey. I had known him as a worthy man in times past, previous to his keeping the tavern. Young as I was, I could well remember the time, when his eyes were not bleared, and his face flushed with unnatural redness, and his whole appearance that of a man enfeebled by disease: all of which characterized him now. Ten years before, he had been a hale and hearty farmer; and with his children growing up around him, all promised a life of enjoyment, and a competency for the period of his own existence, and for starting his sons respectably in life. Unfortunately, he fell into habits of intemperance. Season after season passed away; and each one, as it came, found him a poorer man than that just before it. Everything seemed to go wrong. He attributed it to ill luck, and to the crops being injured by unfavorable weather. But his neighbors found no more harm from these causes than in the years previous, when the tippler was as fortunate as any of them. The truth is, that habits of drunkenness in the head of a family, are like an evil influence—a great dark cloud, overhanging all, and spreading its gloom around every department of the business of that family, and poisoning their peace, at the same time that it debars them from any chance of rising in the world.

So, as matters grew worse, my hapless friend narrowed down the operations of his farm, and opened his dwelling as a country inn. Poor fellow! he was his own best customer. He made out to glean a scanty subsistence from the profits of his new business; but all the old domestic enjoyment and content, seemed fled for ever. The light laugh, and the cheerful chuckle with which he used to toss his infant child in his arms, when [he] returned at evening from his labor, were heard no more. And the cozy and comfortable winter fireside—the great wide hearth, around which they used to cluster when the hail pattered against the small windows from without—where was its comfort now? Alas! while the hearth itself remained in its old place, the happy gatherings were passed away! Many a time, when a young boy, I had stolen from my own home of an evening, to enjoy the vivacity and the mirth of that cheerful fireside. But now, like an altar whose gods and emblems were cast down and forgotten, it was no more the scene of joy, or the spot for the pleasantness of young hearts. The fumes of tobacco, and the strong smell of brandy and gin, defiled its atmosphere; while its huge logs, as they blazed upward, lighted the faces of pallid or bloated inebriates!

The farmer's sons, too, had left him, and gone to seek their living in a more congenial sphere. Intemperance is the parent of peevishness and quarrels, and all uncharitableness. Every day brought new causes of grievance and of dissension. Sometimes, the father was unreasonable, and demanded of his children far more than was consistent with justice. Sometimes, they forgot the respect due from son to parent; for whatever may be the faults of those who give us birth, there is little excuse for thankless ones, whose disobedience to the parental will is indeed sharper than the serpent's tooth. And so the grown up children went away from the family residence, and were thenceforward almost as strangers.

I have been led into an episode. Let me return to the matter more immediately in point to the plot of my narrative. Upon getting into the vehicle, I found that it already had four occupants, whom I had not seen before; as the canvas top had concealed and sheltered them, and they had remained silent during my conversation with the driver and the people of the tavern. Some part of what I learned about these personages, in the course of our journey, I may as well state here.

There was a young man about four or five years older than myself. His name was John Colby. He was a bookkeeper in a mercantile establishment in the city, and from his lively, good-tempered face, one might easily judge that fun and frolic were the elements he delighted in. Colby sat on the same seat with myself, and not many minutes passed away before we were on quite sociable terms with one another.

Back of us sat an elderly country woman, who was going to

visit a daughter. Her daughter, she took occasion to inform us, had married a very respectable citizen about three months previous, and they now lived in good style in the upper part of a two-story house in Broome-street. The woman was evidently somewhat deficient in the perception of the ridiculous—as she herself was concerned; but still, as she *was* a woman, and a mother, and her conversation was quite harmless—no one thought of evincing any sign of amusement or annoyance at her rather lengthy disquisitions upon what, to us, were totally uninteresting topics.

At her side was a middle-aged gentleman, named Demaine. He was dressed with such exceeding neatness that I could not but wonder how he came to ride in so homely a conveyance. Of his character, more will be learned in the subsequent pages.

On the back seat of all, and crowded among a heterogeneous mass of "market truck," sat a gentleman, the last of my four companions. I could occasionally hear him humming a tune to himself, which was proof that he did not feel in any other than a pleasant mood. He was dressed plainly, though I thought richly; and I understood by my friend, the driver, at one of the stopping places, that his rear passenger had come with him from an obscure village, whence there was no other conveyance, and where he had been for sporting purposes.

# II

There stood the Indian hamlet, there the lake
Spread its blue sheet that flashed with many an oar,
Where the brown otter plunged him from the brake,
And the deer drank; as the light gale flew o'er,
The twinkling maize-field rustled on the shore;
And while that spot, so wild, and lone, and fair,
A look of glad and innocent beauty wore,
And peace was on the earth, and in the air,
The warrior lit the pile, and bound his captive there.

Not unavenged—the foeman from the wood
Beheld the deed.

BRYANT

THE journey on which we were all bound, (each of us was going to New-York,) might have been rather monotonous, were it not that after a few miles we most of us allowed the reserve of strangers to melt away, and began to treat one another as familiar acquaintances. My neighbor by the side of the country woman, was the only exception to this. He preserved a stiff pragmatical demeanor, and evidently thought it beneath him to be amused, and quite indecorous to join in the laugh at our little witticisms. Colby and I, however, chatted away, occasionally interchanging a remark with the gentleman on the back seat, whom we found to be quite a fine fellow, according to our notions. Though there was a species of dignity about him which forbade too near an approach of familiarity, there was nothing of that distant haughtiness which characterized our other male passenger.

With the disposition of cheerful hearts, we found a source of pleasure in almost everything. The very slowness and sleepiness of the pace with which our horses jogged along was, the text for many a merry gibe and humorous observation. Entering into the spirit of our gayety, the sportsman in the further seat entertained us with numerous little anecdotes, many of them having reference to scenes and places along the road we were passing. He had, he told us, a fondness for prying into the olden history of this, his native island; a sort of antiquarian taste for the stories and incidents connected with the early settlers, and with the several tribes of Indians who lived in it before the whites came.

I could see, indeed, that the gentleman was quite an enthusiast on the subject, from the manner in which he spoke upon it. He dwelt with much eloquence upon the treatment the hapless red men had received from those who, after dispossessing them of land and home, now occupied their territory, and were still crowding them from the face of their old hunting-grounds.

"The greatest curse," said he, growing warm with his subject—"the greatest curse ever introduced among them, has been the curse of *rum!* I can conceive of no more awful and horrible, and at the same time more effective lesson, than that which may be learned from the consequences of the burning fire-water upon the habits and happiness of the poor Indians. A whole people—the inhabitants of a mighty continent—are crushed by it, and debased into a condition lower than the beasts of the field. Is it not a pitiful thought? The bravest warriors—the wise old chiefs—even the very women and children —tempted by our people to drink this fatal poison, until, as year and year passed away, they found themselves deprived not only of their lands and what property they hitherto owned, but of everything that made them noble and grand as a nation! Rum has done great evil in the world, but hardly ever more by wholesale than in the case of the American savage."

We could not but feel the justice of his remarks. Even our driver, whose red nose spoke him no hater of a glass of brandy, evidently joined in the sentiment.

As we crossed a small creek over which a bridge was thrown, he who had spoken so fervently in behalf of the Indians, pointed us to [look] over the fields in the distance, where we could see quite a large inland sheet of water. He told us it was a lake about two miles broad, and gave us a long and unpronounceable word, which he said was the Indian name for it.

"There is an old tradition," said he—and we could perceive that he was now upon a favorite hobby—"there is a very old tradition connected with this lake, which may perhaps diversify our journey, by the relation."

We all professed our pleasure at the idea of hearing it, and without further preliminary the antiquarian began:

Among the tribes of red men that inhabited this part of the world three hundred years ago, there was a small brave nation, whose hunting-grounds lay adjacent to the eastern shore of that lake. The nation I speak of, like most of its neighbors, was frequently engaged in war. It had many enemies, who sought every means to weaken it, both by stratagem and declared hostility. But the red warriors who fought its battles were very brave; and they had a chief, whose courage and wonderful skill in all the savage arts of warfare, made him renowned through the island, and even on no small portion of the continent itself. He was called by a name which, in our language, signifies "Unrelenting." There were only two dwellers in his lodge—himself and his youthful son; for twenty moons had filled and waned since the chieftain's wife was placed in the burial-ground of her people.

As the Unrelenting sat alone one evening in his rude hut, one of his people came to inform him that a traveller from a distant tribe had entered the village, and desired food and repose. Such a petition was never slighted by the red man; and the messenger was sent back with an invitation for the stranger to abide in the lodge of the chief himself. Among these simple people, no duties were considered more honorable than arranging the household comforts of a guest. Those duties were now performed by the chief's own hand, his son having not yet returned from the hunt on which he had started, with a few young companions, at early dawn. In a little while the wayfarer was led into the dwelling by him who had given the first notice of his arrival.

"You are welcome, my brother," said the Unrelenting.

The one to whom this kind salute was addressed was an athletic Indian, apparently of middle age, and habited in the scant attire of his race. He had the war-tuft on his forehead, under which flashed a pair of brilliant eyes. His rejoinder to his host was friendly, yet very brief.

"The chief's tent is lonesome. His people are away?" said the stranger, after a pause, casting a glance of inquiry around.

"My brother says true, that it is lonesome," answered the other. "Twelve seasons ago the Unrelenting was a happy ruler of his people. He had brave sons, and their mother was dear to him. He was strong, like a cord of many fibres. Then the Spirit Chief snapped the fibres, one by one, asunder. He looked with a pleasant eye on my sons and daughters, and wished them for himself. Behold all that is left to gladden my heart!"

The Unrelenting turned as he spoke, and pointed to an object just inside the opening of the tent.

A moment or two before, the figure of a boy had glided noiselessly in, and taken his station back of the chief. The new-comer seemed of the age of fourteen or fifteen years. He was a noble youth! His limbs never had been distorted by the ligatures of fashion; his figure was graceful as the slender ash, and symmetrical and springy as the bounding stag. It was the chief's son—the last and loveliest of his offspring—the soft-lipped nimble Wind-Foot.

With the assistance of the child, the preparations for their simple supper was soon completed. After finishing it, as the stranger appeared to be weary, a heap of skins was arranged for him in one corner of the lodge, and he laid himself down to sleep.

It was a lovely summer evening. The moon shone, and the stars twinkled, and the million voices of the forest night sounded in the distance. The chief and his son reclined at the opening of the tent, enjoying the cool breeze that blew fresh upon them, and idly flapped the piece of deer-skin that served for their door—sometimes swinging it down so as to darken the apartment, and then again floating suddenly up, and letting in the bright moonbeams. Wind-Foot spoke of his hunt that day. He had met with poor luck, and in a boy's impatient spirit, he peevishly wondered why it was that other people's arrows should hit the mark, and not his. The chief heard him with a sad smile, as he remembered his own youthful traits: he soothed the child with gentle words, telling him that even brave warriors sometimes went whole days with the same ill success as had befallen him.

"Many years since," said the chief, "when my cheek was soft, and my limbs had felt the numbness of but few winters, I myself vainly traversed our hunting-grounds, as you have done to-day. The Dark Influence was around me, and not a single shaft would do my bidding."

"And my father brought home nothing to his lodge?" asked the boy.

"The Unrelenting came back without any game," the other answered; "but he brought what was dearer to him and his people than the fattest deer or the sweetest bird-meat. His hand clutched the scalp of an accursed Kansi!"

The voice of the chief was deep and sharp in its tone of hatred.

"Will my father," said Wind-Foot, "tell——"

The child started, and paused. A sudden guttural noise came from behind them. It seemed between a prolonged grunt and a dismal groan, and proceeded from that part of the tent where the stranger was lying. The dry skins which formed the bed rustled as if he who lay there was changing his position, and then all continued silent. The Unrelenting turned to his son, and proceeded in a lower tone, fearful that their talk had almost broken the sleep of their guest.

"Listen!" said he; "You know a part, but not all of the cause of hatred there is between our nation and the abhorred enemies whose name I mentioned. Longer back than I can remember, they did mortal wrong to your fathers, and your fathers' people. The scalps of two of your own brothers hang in Kansi tents; and I have sworn, boy, to bear for them a never-sleeping hatred.

"On the morning I spoke of, I started with fresh limbs and a light heart to search for game. Hour after hour I roamed the forest with no success; and at the setting of the sun I found myself weary and many miles from my father's lodge. I lay down at the foot of a tree and sleep came over me. In the depth of the night, a voice seemed whispering in my ears—it called me to rise quickly—to look around. I started to my feet, and found no one there but myself; then I knew that the Dream Spirit had been with me. As I cast my eyes about in the gloom, I saw a distant brightness. Treading softly, I approached. The light, I found, was that of a fire, and by the fire lay two figures. Oh, my son, I laughed the quiet laugh of a deathly mind, as I saw who they were. Two of our hated foes—I knew them well—lay sleeping there; a Kansi warrior, and a child, like you, my son, in age. I felt of my hatchet's edge—it was keen as my hate. I crept toward them as a snake crawls through the grass—I bent over the slumbering boy—I raised my tomahawk to strike—but I thought that, were they both slain, no one would carry to the Kansi tribe the story of my deed. My vengeance would be tasteless to me if they knew it not, so I spared the child. Then I glided to the other. His face was of the same cast as the first; so my soul was gladdened more, for I knew they were of kindred blood. I raised my arm—I gathered my strength—I struck, and cleft his dastard brain in quivering halves!"

The chief's speech trembled with agitation. He had gradually wrought himself up to a pitch of loudness and rage; and his hoarse tones, at the last part of his narration, rang croakingly through the lodge.

At that moment the deer-skin at the door was down, and obscure darkness filled the apartment. The next, the wind buoyed the curtain aside again; the rays of the moon flowed in, and all was a halo of light. Spirits of Fear! what sight was that back there! The strange Indian was sitting up on his couch; his ghastly features glaring forward to the unconscious inmates in front, with a look like that of Satan to his antagonist angel. His lips were parted, and his teeth clenched; his neck stretched forward—every vein in his forehead and temples bulged out as if he was suffocating—and his eyes fiery with a look of demoniac hate. His arm was raised, and his hand doubled; each nerve and sinew of them in bold relief. It was an appalling sight, though it lasted only for a moment. The Unrelenting and his son saw nothing of it, their faces being to the front of the tent; in another instant the Indian had sunk back, and was reposing with the skins wrapped round him, and motionless. It was now an advanced hour of the evening. Wind-Foot felt exhausted by his day's travel; so they arose from their seat at the door, and retired to rest. In a few minutes the father and son were fast asleep; but from the darkness which surrounded the couch of the stranger, there flashed two fiery orbs, rolling about incessantly, like the eyes of a wild beast in anger. The lids of those orbs closed not in slumber during that night.

Among the primitive inhabitants who formerly occupied this continent, it was considered very rude to pester a traveller or a guest with questions about himself, his last abode or his future destination. He was made welcome to stay, until he saw fit to go—whether for a long period or for a short one. Thus, the next day, when the strange Indian showed no signs of departing, the chief entertained little surprise, but made his guest quite as welcome; and indeed felt the better pleased at the indirect compliment paid to his powers of giving satisfaction. So the Indian passed a second night in the chieftain's tent.

The succeeding morn, the Unrelenting called his son to him, while the stranger was standing at the tent door. He told Wind-Foot that he was going on a short journey, to perform which and return would probably take him till night-fall. He enjoined the boy to remit no duties of hospitality toward his guest, and bade him be ready there at evening with a welcome for his father. As the Unrelenting passed from the door of his tent, he was surprised to witness a wildness in the stranger's bright black eyes. His attention, however, was given to it but for a moment; he took his simple equipments, and started on his journey.

It was some public business for his tribe that the Unrelenting went to transact. He travelled with an elastic step, and soon arrived at his destined place. Finishing there what he had to do, sooner than he expected, he partook of a slight refreshment and started for home. When he arrived in sight of his people's settlement it was about the middle of the afternoon. The day, though pleasant, was rather warm; and making his way to his own dwelling, the Unrelenting threw himself on the floor. Wind-Foot was not there; and after a little while, the chief rose and stepped to the nearest lodge to make inquiry after him. A woman appeared to answer his questions:

"The young brave," said she, "went away with the chief's strange guest many hours since."

The Unrelenting turned to go back to his tent.

"I cannot tell the meaning of it," added the woman, "but he of the fiery eye bade me, should the father of Wind-Foot ask about him, say to the chief these words: *'Unless your foe sees you drink his blood, that blood is not sweet, but very bitter.'*"

The Unrelenting started, as if a snake had stung him. His lip quivered, and his hand involuntarily moved to the handle of his tomahawk. Did his ears perform their office truly? Those sounds were not new to him. Like a floating mist, the gloom of past years rolled away in his memory, and he recollected that the words the woman had just spoken, were the very ones himself uttered to the Kansi child, whom he had spared in the forest, long, long ago—and sent back to his tribe to tell how and by whom his companion was killed. And this stranger? Ah, now he saw it all! He remembered the dark looks, the mystery and abruptness that marked his guest; and carrying his mind back again, he traced the same features in his face and that of the Kansi boy. Wind-Foot then was in the hands of this man, and the chief felt too conscious for what terrible purpose. Every minute lost might be fatal! He sallied from his lodge, gathered together a dozen of his warriors, and started in search of the child.

All the chief's suspicions were too true. About the same hour that he returned to his village, Wind-Foot, several miles from home, was just coming up to his companion, who had gone on a few rods ahead of him, and was at that moment seated on the body of a fallen tree, a mighty giant of the woods that some whirlwind had tumbled to the earth. The child had roamed with his new acquaintance through one path after another, with the heedlessness of his age; and now, while the Indian sat in perfect silence for many minutes, the boy idly sported near him. It was a solemn place: in every direction around, were the towering fathers of the wilderness —aged patriarchs, that grew up and withered in those solitudes, and shaded underneath them the leaves of untold seasons. At length the stranger spoke:

"Wind-Foot!"

The child, who was but a few yards off, approached at the call. As he came near, he started, and stopped in alarm; for his companion's features were wild, and bent toward him like a panther, about to make the fatal spring. Those dreadfully bright eyes were rolling, and burning with a horrid glitter; and he had the same fearful appearance that has been spoken of as occurring on the first night he spent in the chief's tent. During the moment that passed while they were thus looking at each other, terrible forebodings arose in the child's mind.

"Young warrior," said the Indian, "you must die!"

"The brave stranger is in play," said the other, "Wind-Foot is a little boy."

"Serpents are small at first," the savage replied, "but in a few moons they have fangs and deadly poison. Hearken!

branch from an evil root. I am a Kansi! The boy whom your parent spared in the forest is now become a man. Young warriors of his tribe point to him and say, 'his father's scalp crackles in the dwelling of the Unrelenting, and the tent of the Kansi is bare.' Offspring of my deadliest foe! Ere another sun has travelled over our heads, your blood must fatten the grave of a murdered father."

The boy's heart beat quickly, but the courage of his race did not forsake him.

"Wind-Foot is not a girl," he said. "The son of a chief can die without wetting his cheek by tears."

The savage looked on him for a few seconds with a malignant scowl. Then producing from an inner part of his dress a withe of some tough bark, he stepped to the youth, to bind his hands behind him. It was useless to attempt anything like resistance, for besides the disparity of their strength, the boy was unarmed; while the Indian had at his waist a hatchet, and a rude stone weapon, resembling a poniard. Having his arms thus fastened, the savage, with a significant touch at his girdle, pointed to Wind-Foot the direction he was to travel—himself following close behind.

When the Unrelenting and his people started to seek for the child, and that fearful stranger whom they dreaded to think about as his companion, they were lucky enough to find the trail which the absent ones had made. None except an Indian's eye would have tracked them by so slight and round-a-bout a guide. But the chief's vision seemed sharp with paternal love, and they followed on, winding and on again—at length coming to the fallen tree on which the Kansi had sat. Passing by this, the trail was less devious, and they traversed it with greater rapidity. Its direction seemed to be to the shores of a long narrow lake, which lay between the grounds of their tribe and a neighboring one. So onward they went, swiftly but silently; and just as the sun's red ball sank in the west, they saw its last flitting gleams dancing in the bosom of the lake. The grounds in this place were almost clear of trees—

a few scattered ones only being interspersed here and there. As they came out from the thick woods, the Unrelenting and his warriors swept the range with their keen eyes.

Was it so, indeed? Were those objects they beheld on the grass some twenty rods from the shore, the persons they sought? And fastened by that shore was a canoe. They saw from his posture that the captive boy was bound; and they saw, too, from the situation of things, that if the Kansi should once get him in the boat, and start for the opposite side of the waters, where very possibly some of his tribe were waiting for him, the chances for a release would be hopelessly faint. For a moment only they paused; then the Unrelenting sprang off, like a wolf deprived of her cubs, uttering loud and clear the shrill battle-cry of his nation.

The rest joined in the terrible chorus, and followed him. As the sudden sound was swept along by the breeze to the Kansi's ear, he jumped to his feet, and with that wonderful self-possession which distinguishes his species, was aware at once of the position of the whole affair, and the course he had best pursue. He seized his captive by the shoulder, and ran toward the boat, holding the person of Wind-Foot between himself and those who pursued, as a shield from any weapons they might attempt to launch after him. He possessed still the advantage. They, to be sure, being unincumbered, could run more swiftly; but he had many rods the start of them. It was a fearful race; and the Unrelenting felt his heart grow very sick as the Indian, dragging his child, approached nearer to the water's edge.

"Turn, whelp of a Kansi!" the chief madly cried. "Turn! thou whose coward arm warrest with women and children! Turn, if thou darest, and meet the eye of a full-grown brave!"

A loud taunting laugh of scorn was borne back from his flying enemy, to the ear of the furious father. The savage did not look around, but twisted his left arm, and pointed with his finger to Wind-Foot's throat. At that moment he was within twice his length of the canoe. The boy whom he dragged after him, heard his father's voice, and gathered his energies, faint and bruised as he was, for a last struggle. Ah! vainly he strove: the only result was to loosen himself for a moment from the deathly grip of the Kansi; and his body fell to the ground—though it was useless, for his limbs were bandaged, and he could not rescue himself from his doom. That moment, however, was a fatal one for the Kansi. With the speed of lightning, the chief's bow was up to his shoulder—the cord twanged sharply—a poison-tipped arrow sped through the air—and, faithful to its mission, cleft the Indian's side, just as he was stooping to lift Wind-Foot in the boat. He gave a wild shriek—his life-blood spouted from the wound—and he staggered and fell on the sand. His strength, however, was not yet gone. Hate and measureless revenge—the stronger that they were baffled—raged within him, and appeared in his glaring countenance. Fiend-like glances shot from his eyes, glassy as they were beginning to be with the death damps; and his hand felt to his waistband, and clutched the poniard handle. Twisting his body like a bruised snake, he worked himself close up to the bandaged Wind-Foot. He raised the weapon in the air—he shouted aloud—he laughed a laugh of horrid triumph—and as the death-rattle shook in his throat, the instrument (the shuddering eyes of the child saw it, and shut their lids in intense agony) came down, driven too surely to the heart of the hapless Wind-Foot.

When the Unrelenting came up to his son, the last signs of life were quivering in the boy's countenance. His eyes opened, and turned to the chief; his beautiful lips parted in a smile, the last effort of innocent fondness. On his features flitted a transient lovely look, like a passing ripple of the wave—a slight tremor shook him—and the next moment, Wind-Foot was dead!

# III

Thine is the spring of life, dear boy,
  And thine should be its flowers;
Thine, too, should be the voice of joy,
  To hasten on the hours:
And thou, with cheek of rosiest hue,
  With winged feet, should'st still
Thy sometime frolic course pursue,
  O'er lawn and breezy hill.
Not so! what means this foolish heart,
  And verse as idly vain?
Each has his own allotted part
  Of pleasure and of pain!

HENRY PICKERING

WE were so interested in the legend of the antiquary, that we did not notice how time passed away while it was being related. For some minutes after its conclusion, there was silence among us; for the luckless death of the poor Indian boy seemed to cast a gloom over our spirits, and indispose us for conversation.

As it was now past noon, we began to feel as though we should be none the worse for our dinner. Accordingly, in good time, our driver drew up at a low-roofed public house, and proceeded with great deliberation to ungear his horses, for the purpose of giving them a temporary respite from their labors.

Glad of being able to get out in the open air, and upon our legs once more, myself and Colby (for we had become quite cronies) sprang lightly from the vehicle, and bouncing along the little door-yard, felt quite refreshed at stretching our cramped limbs on the low porch which ran along in front of the house. Demaine got out very leisurely, and, with a cool disdainful look, stood by the front wheels of the wagon, eyeing the house and the people of the place, some of whom now made their appearance. The country woman also made a movement forward. She was a fat and somewhat clumsy dame; and we thought the least Demaine could do would be to offer her some assistance in getting down upon the ground. He stood in such a position himself, that he effectually precluded any one else from offering that assistance. But he continued his contemptuous stare, and paid, apparently, not the least attention to what was going on around him.

Turning around a moment to look at Colby, who called my attention in the room, the next minute my hearing was assailed by a quick cry; and upon looking toward the wagon, I saw that the woman had entangled her dress, and was on the point of falling. A little longer, and she might have been down upon that part of the vehicle just behind the horses, or even under their feet; and yet Demaine, with his arrogant look, offered her no assistance! I sprang toward her; but before I could reach the place, the antiquary had rapidly jumped out upon the ground, and was safely landing her beside him. The incident was a trifling one; but I don't know that I ever, merely from one item of conduct, took such a dislike to any man as I did to Demaine, for that occurrence.

I thought I noticed, during our dinner, that the antiquary regarded Demaine with peculiarly cool and distant demeanor. To us, he was affable and pleasant, and polite in his attentions to the old lady; but though not rude, I am sure the same feelings which took root in my own mind, started in his also.

Upon resuming our journey, the same vivacity and fund of anecdote, which had so agreeably entertained us, from our companion in the back seat, was again in requisition. I don't know how it was, but I felt confident that the antiquary was more than he seemed. His manners were so simple, and at the same time so free from anything like coarseness, that I said to myself, if I should aspire to be a *gentleman,* here would be my model. There was nothing in his conduct from which it might be inferred that he wished to demand your respect; on the contrary, he was quite friendly, and talked about plain things in plain language. Yet he had the stamp of superior station, and an indescribable air of something which told us that he would have been quite as much at home, and quite as unassuming, in the parlors of the richest people of the land. In the course of conversation, it came to be mentioned by me, that I was going to the city for the first time since I was a little child, and that I intended making it my future residence. Whether the antiquary was interested in my remarks, or whether he merely spoke from his natural good-will, I do not know; but he addressed me somewhat after this fashion:

"You are taking a dangerous step, young man. The place in which you are about to fix your abode, is very wicked, and as deceitful as it is wicked. There will be a thousand vicious temptations besetting you on every side, which the simple method of your country life has led you to know nothing of. Young men, in our cities, think much more of dress than they do of decent behavior. You will find, when you go among them, that whatever remains of integrity you have, will be laughed and ridiculed out of you. It is considered 'green' not to be up to all kinds of dissipation, and familiar with debauchery and intemperance. And it is the latter which will assail you on every side, and which, if you yield to it, will send you back from the city, a bloated and weak creature, to die among your country friends, and be laid in a drunkard's grave; or which will too soon end your days in some miserable street in the city itself. It is indeed a dangerous step!"

The kindness of the motives of the speaker, prevented any displeasure I might have felt at being thus addressed by a perfect stranger. Colby whispered to me, that the antiquary was undoubtedly a good fellow, but somewhat too sour in his judgments; which may have been the case, in truth. The subsequent pages, however, will prove the wisdom of his warning upon the subject of intemperance.

As the afternoon waned, and the sun sank in the west, we drew nigher and nigher to our destination. The increasing number of carriages, the houses closer to one another, and the frequent sight of persons evidently just out from the city for a ride, admonished us that we were on the point of entering the great emporium of our western world.

When at last we came upon the paved streets, I was astonished at the mighty signs of life and business everywhere around. It was yet sometime ere sunset, and as the day was fine, numbers of people were out, some of them upon business, and many enjoying an afternoon saunter.

The place at which our conveyance stopped was in Brooklyn, near one of the ferries that led over to the opposite side of the river. We dismounted; glad enough to be at the end of our journey, and quite tired with its wearisomeness. Our passengers now prepared to go to their several destinations. The antiquary took a little carpet bag in his hand, and politely bidding us adieu, made his way for the boat near by. Demaine was more lengthy in his arrangements. He had not much more to carry than the antiquary, but he called a porter, and engaged him to take it down to the landing. The country woman, also, hurried away; eager, no doubt, with parental fondness, to see her child.

Before Colby left me, we spoke for several minutes together. Though we had never seen each other until the morning of that day, a kind of friendship had grown up between us; and as I was in a strange place, with hardly an acquaintance in all its wide limits, it may be imagined I felt in no disposition to dissolve the bands [bonds?] of that friendship. Colby gave me the street and number where I could find him. The place of his business was in Pearl-street; his boarding-house further up town.

"I shall always be glad to see you," said he, "and as you seem to be unused to the town, perhaps you may find me of some advantage. Call and see me to-morrow."

"You may expect me," I answered, and we parted.

And now I was in the city. Here I had come to seek my fortune. What numbers had failed in the same attempt!

It may not be amiss to let the reader into the few simple incidents of my former history. My father had been a mechanic, a carpenter; and died when I was some three or four years old only. My poor mother struggled on for a time—what few relations we had being too poor to assist us—and at the age of eleven, she had me apprenticed to a farmer on Long Island, my uncle. It may be imagined with what agony I heard, hardly twenty months after I went to live with my uncle, that the remaining parent had sickened and died also. The cold indifference of the strangers among whom she lived, allowed her to pass even the grim portals of death before they informed me of her illness. She died without the fond pressure of her son's hand, or the soothing of a look from one she loved.

I continued to labor hard, and fare so too; for my uncle was a poor man and his family was large. In the winters, as is customary in that part of the island, I attended school, and thus picked up a scanty kind of education. The teachers were, however, by no means overburthened with learning themselves; and my acquirements were not such as might make any one envious.

As I approached my nineteenth year, my uncle, who was an honest and worthy man, evidently felt that he was hardly justifiable in keeping me at work in an obscure country town, to the detriment of my future prospects in life. With a liberality therefore, of which many a richer person might be glad to be able to boast, he gave up the two last years of my apprenticeship—and the very two, which perhaps, would have been of more value to him than all the others. He called me to him one day, and addressing me in the kindest terms, informed me, what he felt he ought to do for his brother's child—but which his poverty prevented him from doing. He gave me my choice—whether to go to New York, and see what I could do there for a living, or to remain a while longer with him; not to labor, but to attend school, and perfect myself in some more valuable parts of education. Probably, it would have been far better had I chosen the latter of the two alternatives. But with the anxious and ambitious heart of youth, I immediately determined upon the former.

The matter thus settled, arrangements were soon made—my little stock of clothes packed up in the old valise already introduced to the reader—and receiving with thankfulness from my uncle a small sum of money, which I felt sure he must have cramped himself to bestow on me, I made my adieus to my aunt and my sorrowful cousins, and went my way. The first day of my leaving home, found me at evening, as the reader knows, on the borders of that great city, where I was to take up my abode.

Yes, here I had come to seek my fortune! A mere boy, friendless, unprotected, innocent of the ways of the world—without wealth, favor, or wisdom—here I stood at the entrance of the mighty labyrinth, and with hardly any consciousness of the temptations, doubts, and dangers that awaited me there. Thousands had gone before me, and thousands were coming still. Some had attained the envied honors—had reaped distinction—and won princely estate; but how few were they, compared with the numbers of failures! How many had entered on the race, as now I was entering, and in the course of years, faint, tired, and sick at heart, had drawn themselves out aside from the track, seeking no further bliss than to die. To die! The word is too hard a one for the lip of youth and hope. Let us rather think of those who, bravely stemming the tide, and bearing up nobly against all oppositions, have proudly come off victorious—waving in their hands at last, the symbol of triumph and glory.

What should be *my* fate? Should I be one of the fortunate few? Were not the chances much more against me than they had been against a thousand others, who were the most laggard in the contest? What probability was there, that amid the countless multitude, all striving for the few prizes which Fortune had to bestow, *my* inexperienced arm should get the better of a million others?

Oh, how good a thing it is that the great God who has

placed us in this world—where amid so much that is beautiful, there still exists vast bestowal among men of grief, disappointment, and agony—has planted in our bosoms the great sheet-anchor, Hope! In the olden years, as we look back to our former life, we feel indeed how vain would have been our strife without the support of this benignant spirit.

To be sure, thousands had gone before me, in the struggle for the envied things of existence, and *failed.* But many others had met with *success.* A stout heart, and an active arm, were the great levers that might raise up fortune, even for the poor and unfriended Franklin Evans. In our glorious republic, the road was open to all; and my chance, at least, was as good as that of some of those who had began with no better prospects.

# IV

Stay, mortal, stay! nor heedless thus,
  Thy sure destruction seal:
Within that cup there lurks a curse
  Which all who drink shall feel.
Disease and death, for ever nigh,
  Stand ready at the door;
And eager wait to hear the cry.
Of "Give me one glass more!"

WASHINGTONIAN MINSTREL

When I arose the next morning, and thought over in my mind what it would be better for me to do first, I saw that it was necessary to provide myself with a boarding-house. After breakfast, I crossed the ferry, and purchasing a paper of one of the news-boys, for a penny, I looked over to the column containing advertisements of the places similar to what I wished. I was somewhat surprised to find that every one had the most "airy, delightful location," the very "best accommodations," with "pleasant rooms," and "all the comforts of a home." Some of them informed the reader that there were "no children in the house." These I passed over, determining not to go there; for I loved the lively prattle of children, and was not annoyed as some people pretend to be, by their little frailties.

Noting down upon a memorandum several that I thought might suit me, I started on my voyage of discovery. The first place that I called at was in Cliff street. A lean and vinegar-faced spinster came to the door, and upon my inquiring for the landlady, ushered me into the parlor, where in a minute or two I was accosted by that personage. She was as solemn and as sour as the spinster, and upon mentioning my business, gave me to understand that she would be happy to conclude a bargain with me, but upon several conditions. I was not to stay out later than ten o'clock at night—I was to be down at prayers in the morning—I was never to come into the parlor except upon Sundays—and I was always to appear at table with a clean shirt and wristbands. I took my hat, and politely informed the lady, that if I thought I should like her terms, I would call again.

I next made a descent upon a house, which in the advertisement, was described as offering good conveniences on "very reasonable terms." This I supposed meant that it was a cheap boarding-house. The mistress took me up into an open attic, where were arranged beds of all sorts and sizes. She pointed me to a very suspicious looking one, in a corner, which she said was not occupied. She told me I could have that, and my meals, for three dollars a week, payable punctually on every Saturday night. I did not like the look of the woman, or the house. There was too little cleanliness in both; so I made the same remark at parting as before.

A third and fourth trial were alike unsuccessful. The fifth, I liked the house very well, but upon being informed that all the boarders were men, I determined upon making another trial. I desired to obtain quarters where the society was enlivened with ladies.

Quite tired at length with my repeated disappointments, and more than half suspicious that I was myself somewhat too fastidious, I determined that my next attempt should bring matters to a conclusion. Fortunately, the place I called at, had very few of the objections I found with the others. The landlady seemed an intelligent, rather well-bred woman, and the appearance of the furniture and floors quite cleanly. And here it will perhaps be worth while for me to state, that this item of cleanliness was one which I could not forego, from the effects of my country life. I had been used to see, amid much poverty, the utmost freedom from anything like dirt, dust, or household impurity. And without it, I could not be comfortable in any situation.

I concluded an arrangement with the woman, and told her I should come that very day. I was to have a snug little room in the attic, exclusively for my own use, and was to pay three dollars and a half per week.

Soon after leaving this place, which I gave a good look at when I got outside, lest I might forget it, I went down in Pearl-street to call upon Colby. He was glad to see me, but as it was now the business part of the day, and I saw he had plenty to do, I did not stay but a few minutes. I gave him the street and number of my new residence, and he engaged to call and see me in the evening, when his employments were over.

Who should I meet, as I was coming up from the ferry after having been over to Brooklyn for my valise, but my friend of the day before, the antiquary. He expressed his pleasure at seeing me by a smile, and a few kind words.

"And how do you like the city?" said he.

"I have hardly had an opportunity of finding out much about it yet, sir. But I dare say I shall know more by-and-by."

"Too much," he rejoined, shaking his head—"too much, perhaps. There are a thousand things here, my young friend, which no man is the better for knowing."

He paused, and I knew not exactly what reply to make.

"May I ask what you intend doing in New-York," said he, at length.

"I hardly know myself, sir," I answered; "I have come here with the intention of getting employment. What that may be, will depend a good deal upon my luck. I shall not mind much what I turn my hand to, so that I gain an honest living by it, and a fair chance of bettering myself as I grow older."

"That is a strange way," said my companion, evidently with some interest. "People are not apt to get any employment worth having in this city, if they come here in the way I understand you to say you come."

"I am determined to do my best. Perhaps," I added, for I thought the antiquary showed quite a friendly disposition—

"perhaps, sir, you could suggest something to me in the way of getting a situation?"

My friend looked down upon the ground awhile, and smiling good-humoredly as he raised his face, replied,

"Well, Evans, I possibly may do something for you. Look you: I do not wish to conceal that I am somewhat interested in your case. When but a little older than you, I came to this city, in pretty much the same way that you come now. I was not poor, but was without acquaintances or friends, as you say you are. And though I had money, I received, God knows, but little friendliness from those who might have shown at least some kindness to me: but whose dispositions were not as large as their means, for they were rich. I have, however, lived long enough to do without their friendship, and I don't know what reason there is that I should not give you a helping hand. Perhaps what I may do for you may not be much, and may not cost me anything. So much the more scope for your own exertions, and honor to you if you hew out your fortune for yourself. Here is my card," and he handed it to me: "come to me to-morrow morning at eleven. I am punctual, and shall expect you to be the same; and perhaps you will not regret the chance acquaintance you made in the market-wagon. Good day."

I could hardly return the salutation, so pleased was I at the turn events were taking. To be sure, I did not know the nature of the business my friend would employ me in, but it *was* employment, and that was the first stepping-stone to the heights that lay above. I looked at the card; upon it was written, "*Stephen Lee,*–, Exchange Place." I carefully deposited it in my breast pocket, and with a lighter step wended on to my new boarding-house.

Whether it was that I had gained confidence since my interview with Mr. Lee, or from some other cause, I felt myself very little abashed at sitting down, for the first time in my life, at dinner with some twenty well-bred ladies and gentlemen. Though many of the observances were somewhat new to me, and one or two of my nearest neighbors, plainly saw, and felt amused, at my unsophisticated conduct in some respects; I believe I came off, upon the whole, with tolerable credit.

I had an opportunity, too, of seeing who were the really well-bred people of the house. For those possessed of the truest politeness will never deign to wound the feelings of one in their company, by showing that they notice his deficiencies, and are entertained at his ignorance and awkwardness. On the contrary, they would rather do like that greatest of rakes, and of gentlemen, George IV., who, when some court ladies, at tea, simpered at a couple of unfashionable companions for pouring their tea in their saucers, instead of drinking it from their cups; poured his also into the saucer, and thus commended it to his royal lips, that they might not be mortified by the mirth of the rude ones.

At night, Colby, according to his promise, paid me a visit. He was much pleased when I told him of my encounter with Lee, and of his promise to me. He told me, when I showed him the card, that he had frequently heard of that personage, who was a merchant of much reputation and no small wealth. Colby congratulated me on my luck, and jokingly told me, he should not be surprised to see me one day the owner of warehouses and the head of [a] great business.

"But come," said he, "this is dull fun here. Let us go out and cruise a little, and see what there is going on."

"Agreed," said I. "I shall like it of all things."

So we took our hats and sallied forth from the house.

After strolling up and down one of the most busy streets several times, I became a little more used to the glare of the lamps in the windows, and the clatter and bustle which was going on around me. How bright and happy everything seemed! The shops were filled with the most beautiful and costly wares, and the large, clear glass of the show-windows flashed in the brilliancy of the gas, which displayed their treasures to the passers-by. And the pave was filled with an eager and laughing crowd, jostling along, and each intent on some scheme of pleasure for the evening. I felt confused for a long time with the universal whirl, until at length, as I said, the scene grew a little more accustomed, and I had leisure to think more calmly upon what I saw.

In a little while, Colby asked me if I did not wish to hear some fine music and drink a glass of wine. I assented, and we entered a beautifully furnished room, around which little tables were placed, where parties were seated drinking and amusing themselves with various games. We took our station at the first vacant seats, and called for our drinks. How delicious everything seemed! Those beautiful women—warbling melodies sweeter than ever I had heard before, and the effect of the liquor upon my brain, seemed to lave me in happiness, as it were, from head to foot!

Oh, fatal pleasure! There and then was my first false step after coming in the borders of the city—and *so soon* after, too! Colby thought not, perhaps, what he was doing—but still he was very much to blame. He knew I was young, fond of society, and inexperienced; and it would have been better for me had he ushered me amid a pest-house, where some deadly contagion was raging in all its fury.

I tremble now as I look back upon the results which have sprung from the conduct of that single night, as from one seed of evil. Over the lapse of ten years I gaze, and the scene comes back to me again in the most vivid reality. I can remember even the colors of the chequerboard, and the appearance of the little table, and the very words of some of the songs that were sung. We drank—not once only, but again and again.

Yes, with a singular distinctness, the whole appearance of the room, and of the men with their hats on and cigars in their mouths, that sat all about, are as plain before my eyes as though they were painted in a picture there. It was all new to me then. A hundred more exciting scenes have passed over my head since, and have left no impression, while this is marked as with a steel pencil upon the tablets of my memory.

I remember being struck with the appearance of one poor fellow in a corner. He probably was not much older than myself; yet his face was bloated, his eyes inflamed, and he leaned back in that state of drowsy drunkenness which it is so disgusting to behold. I presume his companions—those who had made merry with him until he was brought to this stage of degradation—had left him in scorn; and there he sat, or rather supported himself in the corner, not half awake, and the subject of many a gibe and light laugh. Was it not a warning to me? And yet I was not warned.

After a time, some of the white-aproned subordinates of the place came to him, roughly broke his slumbers, and put him forth from the place. Miserable man! Without doubt, he now sleeps the sleep which no jostle can awaken, and which no curl of the lip, or gibe of the scoffer, can start from its dark repose. He must have died the death of the drunkard!

Colby saw at length that he had been too heedless with me. Used as he was to the dissipation of city life, he forgot that I was from the country, and [had] never in my life before engaged in such a scene of *pleasure*.

With some difficulty preserving the steadiness of my pace, as we left the room, I took his arm, and he walked with me toward my residence. Indeed, if he had not done so, I question whether I should have reached it; for my head swam, and the way in the night was somewhat difficult to find. Leaving me at the door, my companion bade me good night, and departed.

I entered, took a light from a number which were left upon a table in the hall for the use of the boarders, and slowly ascended the stairs to my room. My slumbers were deep and unbroken. So were those of the preceding evening, and yet the nature of the two was widely different. The former was the repose of health and innocence—the latter, the dull lethargy of *drunkenness*.

# V

All is not gold that glitters.

OLD PROVERB

THE reflections which operated in my mind the next morning are not a sufficiently tempting theme for me to dwell upon. I can hardly say that shame and remorse possessed me to such a degree, as to counterbalance the physical discomfort which weighed painfully upon every part of my frame.

In the course of the forenoon, I visited my antiquarian merchant friend, Mr. Lee. He had not forgotten me, but was as good as his word. His own establishment, he said, already employed a sufficiency of clerks and attendants whom he could not turn out without doing them injustice. He had made inquiries, and informed me that a Mr. Andrews, a gentleman doing business in Wall street, with whom he was slightly acquainted, might be able to give me a situation.

My patron wrote a note, addressed to Andrews, which I carried to that personage. I found him in a handsome granite edifice, in a back room furnished sumptuously, out of which opened another, fronting on the street. It was a bank. Numerous people were constantly coming and going, upon business; everything was transacted with a quiet easy air, and without much bustle, though I could see that the matters which were discussed involved the value of thousands.

What conceivable situation Mr. Lee could have had in view for me there, I could not imagine; but I was soon undeceived. Mr. Andrews looked over the note, and called me to him. He was a thin, black-eyed, rather delicate-looking man, and had a completely professional appearance. He told me he was a lawyer, and that his connection with the institution in which I now saw him did not prevent him from attending to his other avocations. He wanted some one as kind of clerk, porter, and errand boy—three in one—to take care of his office while he was absent. The office was in an upper part of the same street.

I readily agreed to accept the terms which Andrews proposed, and he desired me to commence my duties on the morrow. As I took my departure from the place, who should I see in front, with a quill behind his ear, but my market-wagon acquaintance, Demaine. I accosted him with the salutation of the day, but he made a very slight and cool answer; and as I did not care much about his good-will, I went forth without further parley.

Somewhat at a loss what to do with myself, I walked down to Colby's place of business, and made him promise to call upon me again that evening, as he had the preceding one.

"And how have you felt to-day?" said he, smiling mischievously; "you country boys cannot hold up under a few glasses, like us of the city."

I blushed, as I brought to mind the folly I had committed, and internally thought I could never be guilty of it again.

"I know," answered I, "that there are many things in which you will find me rather awkward. But my very visit here, to ask you again to-night, proves that I am willing to get knowledge."

Knowledge! Better would it have been for me had I remained in ignorance through the whole course of my life, than [to have] attained to *such* knowledge.

When Colby came in the evening, and we started out to walk as before, I felt determined not to go in the musical drinking-house again. But I don't know how it was, the very first proposition my companion made to that effect, found me a willing listener. We entered, and called for our drinks.

It was indeed a seductive scene. Most of the inmates were young men; and I noticed no small number quite on the verge of boyhood. They played the same as the rest, and tossed off glasses of liquor, without apparently feeling any evil effects from it. Little as I knew of the world, I felt that there was something wrong here. The keeper of the house was not an American. He made his appearance now and then among the company, smiling and bowing, and highly pleased, no doubt, that shillings were pouring into his pockets with such profitable rapidity.

And the music again! How sweet it sounded out, combined with the fascinating looks of the females who sang. I was completely enthralled, and drank deeper even than the night before.

In the course of the evening some little incidents happened, which served as a proof of the truth of the old proverb, which declares that glittering things may not be of the value they seem. It happened thus. Colby and myself, accompanied by a friend of my friend's, whom we met at the drinking-room, determined to go on to the theatre that evening, and accordingly did so. The house was crowded. Beautiful women and elegant men—moustached dandies and lively youth—brilliant fashionables of all varieties, combined to render the scene exhilarating and splendid. And the music from the orchestra, now soft and subdued, now bursting out with notes of thunder—how delicious it glided into the ear! The curtain drew up and the play began. It was one of those flippant affairs, that pretend to give a picture of society and manners among the exclusive. The plot worse than meagre—the truthfulness of the scene a gag, which ought not to have excited aught but ridicule—the most nauseous kind of mock aristocracy tinging the dialogue from beginning to end—yet it was received with applause, and at the conclusion, with vociferous and repeated cheers! The manager had printed upon his bills that London was pleased with it, and that one of the scenes represented life as in the private parlor of an English Duke—with the curtains, carpets, and drapery of the parlor, as good as real! I blushed for the good sense of my countrymen.

In the farce which followed, one of the characters was a wild hoyden of a girl. It was done very agreeably by one of the actresses, whose beauty excited my admiration to no small degree. So much indeed was I fascinated with her, that I expressed my opinion in terms which the liquor I had drank just before by no means contributed to render less strong. I vowed that if I could see her, side by side, and speak to her, I would give the world. Mitchell, the one who made the third of our party, listened to me for some time with a kind of sober surprise; and then, giving a wink to Colby, told me he was acquainted with the actress who had pleased me so much, and would introduce me to her that very evening, if I desired. I thanked him a thousand times.

In the interval between the acts, my eyes were attracted by the figure of a young gentleman in the stagebox, (we sat in the pit,) who seemed to me a perfect pattern of perfection in his dress and manners—in fact, a gentleman of the highest order. I saw Mitchell looking at him also.

"Do you know him?" said I.

"Yes," he answered.

"A fine looking fellow," said I.

He assented.

When the play was over, we went out. Along by the theatre there were the glaring gas lights of several fashionable refectories.

"Gentlemen," said our companion, "suppose we go down here and get some oysters."

We agreed, and down we went.

While waiting in our little box, Mitchell called one of the men in attendance:

"John, bring us a bottle of Port."

The wine was brought.

"Mr. Evans," said Mitchell to me, "do you know I have a fancy always to be served by a particular individual in this refectory? Just notice the man's face, now, and tell me what you think of my taste."

When the waiter came again, in obedience to our companion's call, he held him in talk several minutes about some trivial details respecting the cooking of the articles we had ordered. When he went out, I looked up in Mitchell's face—

"Why," said I, "that—that—that man is the very fellow?"

"What very fellow?"

"He is the picture of the gentleman we saw in the boxes at the theatre!"

"I dare say he is the person; in fact, I know he is."

I changed the subject, and we finished our oysters.

"And now," said Mitchell to me, "if your friend Colby will wait here five minutes, I will introduce you to the actress."

My mistake in regard to the *fashionable gentleman* had taught me a lesson, and my country life had taught me also to keep better hours. So I would have excused myself, but Mitchell seemed anxious that I should go with him.

"It's but a step," said he.

So we walked round the block, into a dirty alley leading to the rear of the theatre. Mitchell told me he had the *entrée* there (to the theatre, I mean, not the alley) and in we walked.

I pass over my stares of wonder, and my running aslant dungeon walls, castles, and canvas palaces. We reached an open space, on one side, where there were quite a number of persons idling. At a little table sat a woman, eating some cheese and thick bread, and drinking at intervals from a dingy pewter mug, filled with beer. She was coarse—her eyes had that sickly bleared appearance, which results from the constant glitter of strong light upon them; her complexion was an oily brown, now quite mottled with paint, and her feet and ankles were encased in thick ill-blacked shoes.

Mitchell went up to the table, (I leaning on his arm), and engaged in chit chat with the delectable creature. He introduced me. I was thunderstruck! *She* was my charmer, of the hoyden in the farce! Her voice was coarse and masculine, and her manners on a par with her voice.

After ten minutes [of] conversation, we bade the lady good night, and wended our way back to Colby, whom we found waiting for us. Neither myself nor Mitchell alluded to the subject, and Colby, no doubt understanding how matters stood, did not mention it either.

The occurrences of the night, I may as well confess, taught me to question the reality of many things I afterward saw; and reflect that, though to appearance they were showy, they might prove, upon trial, as coarse as the eating-house waiter, or the blear-eyed actress. I lost also some of that reverence, and that awkward sense of inferiority, which most country folk, when they take up their abode in this brick-and-pine Babel, so frequently show—and which, by the way, is as amusing to the observers as it is unfair to themselves.

# VI

Strange that such difference there should be
'Twixt tweedle-dum and tweedle-dee.

In the course of a few weeks I became quite at home in my new situation, in the office of Andrews. He treated me very civilly always, though of course he never made any approach to friendliness. I could not expect it, in the situation I occupied.

Under the auspices of my friend Colby, I became pretty well used to city life; and before the winter passed away, I could drink off nearly as much strong liquor as himself, and feel no inconvenience from it. My employer, Mr. Andrews, had become so well satisfied with my performance of my duties, that he advanced me somewhat above my original situation. I had now none of the more menial services to perform. An Irishman, named Dennis, was engaged to act as porter, and to make the fires, open and shut the office, and so on. Andrews occasionally employed him to do business also for the financial institution of which he was an officer.

There is hardly much need that I should detain the reader with a minute account of this part of my career. Though I knew it not at the time, it was the downward career of a drunkard! I concealed from Andrews, as a matter of course, my habits of intemperance, and attended with tolerable carefulness to my duties during the day. Through Colby's means, I soon obtained a wide circle of acquaintance, mostly young men in the same walk of life with ourselves, and having the same habits. We used frequently to go round of nights from place to place, stopping every now and then at some bar-room, and taking a drink all round. This we used to call a "red circle." How appropriate a name that was, the reader can judge for himself.

And about this time (I had lived nearly six months in my situation with Andrews) an incident occurred, which had an important bearing upon my future course of life. Though I saw my good benefactor, Mr. Lee, but seldom, I was not ungrateful for the kindness he had shown me, and often wished that there might be some way of repaying it. One evening, when I had finished my supper, and was going up to my room to prepare for a visit to the theatre, which I had engaged to attend that night with Colby and a party of friends, the landlady handed me a note, which had been left for me during the day. Quite curious to know who could have written to me, and what about, I opened it hastily, and read the following:

*—Exchange Place, Tuesday Morning.*

*Dear Young Friend,*

*The interest I have taken in your welfare, has by no means grown cold, though of late I have not seen you, or had any opportunity of showing my good will. The particular reason of my writing is, that one of my clerks has lately left me; his situation, I think, would be an agreeable one for you, and if you choose to accept it, it is at your service. The salary is $800 per year.*

*Give your present employer a couple* [of] *weeks notice, before you leave him, in order that he may have an opportunity of getting some one in your place. At the end of that time come to me, and I will induct you in your new duties. If this proposition meets your approval, write me to that effect as soon as convenient.*

*Stephen Lee.*

I was quite overjoyed! Not only was the stipend offered me by my old friend more than twice as much as that I received from Andrews, but then I should be in the service of a man I loved, instead of one whom, at best, I could look upon with no stronger feeling than indifference. I sat down immediately, and indited a grateful acceptance of Mr. Lee's offer.

My duties at Andrews', of late, had not been, to tell the truth, of the most pleasant description. We found out, after

Dennis had been with us awhile, that he had an unfortunate habit of tippling, which sadly interfered with his efficiency at work. For my own part, I could not conscientiously find fault with him, and therefore concealed his mistakes as much as possible. But they became so glaring at length, that they could not be hidden, and Andrews discharged him. Dennis frequented a little drinking-shop, which was in one of the streets on my way home, and there I often saw him afterward. So that my own labors were now as heavy as when I first commenced them.

Besides, I occasionally saw things which looked very suspicious, in connection with Andrews' business arrangements. I heard rumors too, in my intercourse with the neighboring clerks, which by no means increased my opinion for my employer's honesty. Those who were supposed to be at home in such affairs, more than hinted that he would before long be summarily removed from his station in the moneyed establishment, before alluded to in these pages. It was asserted also, that Andrews had lately used immense sums of money, the origin of which no one could tell. So I felt not at all grieved at the idea of finding another master, and gave the notice premonitory which Mr. Lee desired, with but ill-concealed gratification.

Some days after, as I was passing down to the office from my breakfast, I saw Dennis, the discharged porter, come out of the little groggery I have mentioned. He stepped forward, and stood upon the curb-stone, looking down upon the ground, very miserable to all appearance. Dennis had gone from bad to worse, until he was now at the very lowest stage of degradation. Though I saluted him, I could hardly conceal my disgust at his filthy and bloated looks! How little did I think, that one day might find me so little removed from his present condition! Perhaps it will not be without a wholesome moral, if I finish this chapter with the relation of poor Dennis's subsequent conduct that day, and [as] an off-set of the doings of another personage, who has figured somewhat in my narrative —as those occurrences subsequently came to my knowledge.

At the early hour I saw him, Dennis was passing through the agonies which mark the period immediately after a fit of intoxication. Pain and hunger racked him in the corporeal frame; despair, mortification and disgust with himself burnt in his heart. He felt that he was a degraded man. With an unwonted bitterness, thoughts of many chances neglected—of weeks spent in riot—of the scorn of the world—and the superciliousness of those called respectable—cut at his heart with a sharp grief. Heaving an inward groan, he started off, and passed down a by-street, to walk away, if possible, such fearful reflections.

Nearly an hour, he rapidly traversed, at hap-hazard, the narrowest and darkest ways he could pick; for he did not wish to be seen. Then his appetite became acute, and he wished for food. Wishing, merely, was vain; and he had not a single cent. Poor creature! In the preceding two days, he had not eaten a single meal. Should he beg? Should he ask for work? His suspicious appearance might subject him to denial; besides, the emergency was one not to be postponed. In an evil moment Dennis yielded to the tempter. He saw, in a small grocery, some bread piled upon a barrel top. He entered, and while the owner was busy at a back shelf, the ravenous man purloined a loaf and made off with it. The keeper of the grocery saw him as he went out, discovered the theft, and pursued the criminal. He was brought back, a police officer called, and the bread found upon him.

So the thief was taken off to prison, and being arraigned a few hours afterward, was summarily convicted, and sentenced to the customary place, just out of the city; there to remain for several days, at hard labor and confinement.

During the same hour wherein these things were being transacted, in another and distant part of the town, sat a gentleman in a parlor. The carpet was very rich, the curtains glossy silk, and the chairs heavy mahogany. The person who sat there was Andrews, my master. On a table before him lay some written papers. By the opposite side of the table, and just about to depart, stood a second gentleman, elegantly attired, and with a lofty look, which spoke of pride within.

"The time is as favorable now," said Andrews, in reply to something his companion had spoken, "as it ever was. Besides, we must make hay while the sun shines. Who knows whether we shall have the chance, five days from this?"

"And yet you are not willing to take the bold steps," rejoined the other; "the transfer ought to have been made a week ago."

"Are you sure it can be made without the others knowing it?" said Andrews.

"As easy as speak," was the answer; "they never examine."

"But they *might* examine."

"I tell you, only pay them a handsome dividend, and they'll rest easy any length of time."

Andrews put his finger under his chin, and looked down a moment abstractedly.

"Have you not determined yet?" asked the person standing.

"Long ago, sir—long ago," was Andrews' reply. "But it is a dangerous game, and should be played cautiously."

"Well, shall we take this step, or no?"

Andrews raised up his head; his dark eye twinkled as it met the glance of his companion, and the two looked at each other a minute. There was evil fraternity in that look. Then Andrews bent his head two or three times without speaking. The other understood him. He smiled, and turning, left the apartment.

A person looking on as they parted would hardly have thought them to be aught else than two respectable citizens—yet were they two most consummate scoundrels. It was indeed too true—the host of rumors I had heard about my employer's honesty. The situation he occupied, he turned to account, by schemes which were nothing more or less than swindling; and his well-dressed companion was of kindred spirit with himself. He had now come to have a private conference with Andrews, and the subject of that conference was a scheme for making a splendid fortune jointly, by means of the peculiar facilities for cheating possessed by both. A long time ago, the plan had been marked out; and now the hour was nigh, to strike the finishing stroke.

It would be painful to describe, as it would also be to read, all the villainy, the deceit, the underhand swindling, and the imposition which these two wicked men had followed, and were on the eve of closing. In all their rascality, however, they acted warily—with the wisdom of the serpent. They knew that whatever might be the execrations of people, the *law* could not touch them. Opinions, too, might be bought: defence and character might be bought. And what, that it was possible to buy, might they not purchase?

In the course of the succeeding week, the conspiracy worked its way out. The bubble burst! The master hands had arranged things well, and they triumphed.

Yet was the tempest a terrible one. Widows, left with a narrow competence; young children; sick people, whose cases were hopeless, but who might languish on for many years; sailors, away upon the ocean; fishermen, whose earnings were scant and dearly bought; mechanics; young men just commencing business; economical doctors and clergymen in their novitiate; all these, and hundreds more, had either deposited sums of money in the institution, or were sufferers by its bankruptcy in other ways. Many lost their all. There was one woman, a widow, an energetic country trader, the mother of a large family, which she supported by her business habits, who had come to the city with what was for her quite a large sum—all she was worth, and some borrowed funds besides. Her intent was to purchase a heavy stock of goods, for sale the subsequent season. For security, she had her money placed in the vaults of the institution—and lost every cent!

It would be almost an endless effort to tell who was injured. All classes, all ranks, all occupations, felt more or less of the withering blight.

But the tempest blew over at last. The two men who had provoked it, went out still among their fellow-men, with forms erect, and with smooth smiles. He of the dark eye was just finishing, a few miles from the city, a palace-like residence, of great size and beauty. Now he had it furnished with the most sumptuous luxury. Cost and pains were not spared, until Desire had no further room for wishing. Here this rich man settled himself; and here, when he had become a little used to his grandeur, so that it did not sit awkwardly upon him, he determined to give a superb entertainment. Preparations were accordingly made; scientific cooks were engaged; foreign delicacies purchased, and the most exquisite dishes prepared.

The hour and the company arrived; and the master of the feast looked around with a smile, as each one seated himself at his appointed place. They ate, and drank, and made merry. Delight, and Friendliness, and Content, seemed the presiding spirits of the banquet.

After awhile, when their glasses were filled with rich wine, it was proposed that they should have a toast. So a benevolent-looking elderly gentleman rose, and after speaking a few minutes, to the purport that he felt sure those present would all cordially join him, he raised his glass aloft—his example being followed by the others, and said—

"*Even-handed laws*—which, in our glorious republic, dispense to all impartially their due."

When the revellers heard this sentiment, they clinked their glasses together, and raised a peal which made the lofty ceiling ring again. Then a second, and then a third—which was a louder and gladder peal than either of the others.

And at the same moment that the echoes died away, there was, about a mile off, a human soul writhing in its final struggle. It was that of the poor drunkard Dennis, who stole the loaf in his hunger, and had been sent to expiate his crime in toil and imprisonment. The dissipation of years had made him weak; and he could not bear up against the exposure, joined with hard work. But his task-maker was merciless; and as long as the wretched man could stand, he was kept laboring. At last, he fell very ill. Who would medicine a rascally jail-bird? He went on from bad to worse, and was soon in a dying condition.

Before the splendid dinner party returned to their homes that night, the corpse of the *convicted* thief lay cold and clayey upon the prison floors.

# VII

"Look not upon the wine when it is red!"

After I had been a while in my situation at Mr. Lee's store, I thought I might safely indulge myself in adding a little to my expenses. I made improvements both in my style of living, and in my dress. The new boarding-house in which I took up my quarters, was in the upper part of the town. Colby came to see me quite often, as usual. The reader probably, by this time, has gained no small insight into the character of my friend. He was by no means a bad man; and yet his early habits, and giving way to temptation, had brought him to be anything else but a fit companion for a country youth, just beginning life in the city.

One morning, while I was attending to my usual duties in the counting-room, a stranger, with a dark and swarthy complexion, came in and asked for Mr. Lee. He was not in at the time; and thinking that the business of the dark-faced personage was very likely some trifling affair, I told him that my employer was away, but would probably return in a half-hour, or less. The stranger paused a moment, with a troubled expression upon his countenance; then drew from his breast-pocket a couple of sealed documents, and handed them to me.

"Give these papers," said he, "to your master, the moment he arrives. They are of more consequence than you know, and I would that I could have delivered them to his own hands."

"I will do as you desire," said I, laying the papers up in a little partition on the desk.

A few minutes afterwards, I learned from one of my fellow-clerks that Mr. Lee had gone out that morning, leaving word that he would not be back till the close of the day. I thought of the stranger's parting injunction; but he was gone some time, and could not be informed how the fact really was. After all, perhaps the documents might be of no weighty moment, and I reflected no more upon the subject.

On my way down from dinner, Colby met me in the street. "This is lucky," he exclaimed, seizing me by the hand. "We have made up a fine party for the play to-night, and you must promise to be one of us."

"With pleasure," was my reply; "nothing could delight me more."

So it was all arranged that, when the hour arrived, they should call upon me, and we would all go together.

We did not close our store as early as usual that evening, in consequence of our employer's absence. Though doing an extensive business, he was a man very careful of the details, and was in the practice of being in his counting-room until the last moment. We waited therefore until the very evening, and the neighbors all around had shut up, and left us quite solitary. As the porter was making the usual arrangements of closing, Mr. Lee returned. He looked around him a moment, remarked that he did not know as his presence there was necessary, and was on the point of departing. So selfish was I, that though at that moment the remembrance of the swarthy stranger, and his letters, came to my mind, I debated a moment whether I should give them to Mr. Lee, as that would detain us some minutes longer. I was in haste to get home, that I might be ready in time for our visit to the theatre. Happily, however, duty triumphed.

"I had nearly forgot, sir," said I, "these papers were left here this morning, by a man who desired that you might get them as soon as possible."

Mr. Lee took them, and opened them. The very moment he began to read, I could see that he was deeply interested. After finishing one, he perused the other with the same eagerness. And thus a second time, with a slower and more careful manner, he read over both the letters again, from beginning to end.

"It's a lucky thing, Evans," said he, "that you did not miss giving me these. Not for half my fortune would I have been without them this very evening."

He then explained to me, that he had of late been engaged in some mercantile speculations at the south, which proved a failure. Some traders with whom he had intercourse there, were becoming alarmed, and demanded certain moneys, or their value, which Mr. Lee was bound to pay; but which, it had been the understanding, were to remain uncalled for, for several months yet. A statement of this sudden demand was forwarded by Mr. Lee's agent, with a sorrowful acknowledgment that he had not the wherewithal to meet it, and asking directions for his conduct. The swarthy southerner, who was a planter, come to the north on business, was going to leave the city the next morning, at an early hour, and prompt action was therefore necessary.

Mr. Lee immediately sat down and wrote to his agent, directing where and how he could obtain the needed funds. He enjoined him to pay the liabilities the moment they were called for, as he would rather be at the expense of them, twice over, than have his reputation and fair name as a merchant put in danger. Having made up and endorsed his reply, he gave it into my hands, with the address of the planter, who was to take it on, telling me to call at his hotel in the course of the evening, and place it in his hands. I promised to do so, of course, and went home to my supper.

As it was now quite in the evening, I had hardly finished my meal before my companions came, according to arrangement, to take me with them to the play. I debated a little while whether I had not better postpone my evening's enjoyment, as I had the planter's letter to carry. But I feared they would suspect that I did not like their companionship; and determined, in my own mind, to go out between some of the earlier acts of the piece, and convey my message.

I went to the theatre. We enjoyed ourselves highly, for the performances were creditable, and each of us naturally fond of that species of amusement, and moreover, in great spirits. As the first piece was one I had long wished to see acted, I concluded not to go until that was finished. Then there was to come a dance, which one of my companions praised so highly that I was determined to stay and see that also. And then the intermission was so very short that, before I knew it, the curtain was up, and the actors on in the after-piece. Feeling that I was not doing right, I made a bold push, and bade my companions good night, if I should not see them again, telling them that I had some business to transact for my employer. They laughed at me, stating the improbability of such a thing, at that time of night. If ever there was anything that annoyed me, it was to be suspected of trying to sneak out from the truth by a kind of back-door, as it were. Accordingly, when they promised that if I would wait until the end of the first act, they would all go with me, I sat down again by them. I knew I was culpable, and yet I had not resolution of mind enough to break away.

We went from the theatre. On our way to the hotel, we were to pass one of our favorite drinking-places, where, as we came off against the entrance, we heard the inmates stamping and applauding at a great rate. There was evidently something more than usual going on, so one of our party insisted that we should step in and have a look.

"Only one moment," said he, "and then we will walk on with Evans."

But the moment stretched on to minutes, and the minutes to almost half an hour; at the end of which time we were snugly seated round a table, imbibing fragrant liquors through long glass tubes. And with the contents of the first glass, came a total disregard of anything but the pleasure of drink. Forgetful of my own duty—of my master's honor, and the crisis which would turn against him, if I continued sitting there a little while longer, I drank, and drank, and drank;

until, as the night advanced, lost to the slightest vestige of remembrance with regard to the pacquet, I was the wildest and most exhilarated of the party.

What fire burnt in my brain! I laughed, and with garrulous tongue, entertained those about me with silly stories, which the quantity of liquor they had taken, alone prevented them from being nauseated with. All around us were the scenes which belonged to such a place, and which I have partly described before. The music went on, but we heard it no longer. The people talked, and the dice rattled, but we heeded them not. The Demon of Intemperance had taken possession of all our faculties, and we were his alone.

A wretched scene! Half-a-dozen men, just entering the busy scenes of life, not one of us over twenty-five years, and there we were, benumbing our faculties, and confirming ourselves in practices which ever too surely bring the scorn of the world, and deserved disgrace to their miserable victims! It is a terrible sight, I have often thought since, to see *young men* beginning their walk upon this fatal journey! To reflect that those faculties which have been given us by God, for our own enjoyment, and the benefit of our fellows, are, at the very outset rendered useless, and of not so much avail as the instinct of the very beasts. To know that the blood is poisoned, and that the strength is to be broken down, and the bloom banished from the cheek, and the lustre of the eye dimmed, and all for a few hours' sensual gratification, now and then—is it not terrible! If there were no other drawback, the mere physical prostration which follows a fit of drunkenness were enough. But to the young, it saps the foundations, not only of the body's health, but places a stigma for the future on their worldly course, which can never be wiped out, or concealed from the knowledge of those about them.

# VIII

Yet sense and passion held them slaves,
  And lashed them to the oar,
Till they were wrecked upon their graves,
  And then they rose no more.
Oh! God of mercy, make me know
  The gift which thou hast given;
Nor let me idly spend it so,
  But make me fit for Heaven!

CHRISTIAN EXAMINER

READER, I am coming to the dark and cloudy part of my fortunes. I would that I had not to tell what you will see in the following pages—but a sentiment of good-will for my fellows, prompts the relation. I think that by laying before them a candid relation of the dangers which have involved me, and the temptations which have seduced me aside, the narrative may act as a beacon light, guiding their feet from the same fearful hazards.

There is no need that I should pause here to dwell on my meeting with my benefactor Lee, and the shame with which I acknowledged my guilt, and gave him back his letter. But great as was my fault, I was hardly prepared for his storm of anger. I did not know how much he worshipped his good name among the mercantile world, or I might have been better prepared for it. He had jealously guarded his professional honor, as the apple of his eye; and now there was no escape. The mails to the distant place were very irregular; and besides, a letter to that town where his agent resided, would not reach it in time, now, if there were no impediment.

Though conscious of my remissness, the irritability, which is one of the results of intemperate habits, caused me in the course of our interview, to attempt an excuse for my conduct. High words arose—in the end I was insolent, and Mr. Lee bade me leave the place and never enter it again! I departed, telling him he should be obeyed.

Dearly, during that day, and many subsequent ones, did I repent my folly. How often did I curse that miserable weakness of my mind, which led me to yield to the slightest opening of temptation!

And what was to be done now, for a living? Some employment must be had—I could not starve. Though my salary had been quite liberal, I had spent every cent, and with the exception of a small sum, due me on a back account, I owned not a dollar in the world. Will it be believed, that, in this strait, I was besotted enough to run into the very jaws of the lion? I accidentally learned that the proprietor of a second-rate hotel, where I had in times past been in the habit of going, was in want of a bar-keeper. I made application for the place, and, after some demur, was accepted. But the scenes which I witnessed there, and the duties my situation obliged me to perform, were too repulsive, even for my callous heart: and at the end of a fortnight I left my place.

During my avocations there, I saw many an occurrence, which, had I possessed true judgment, might have served as a sufficient warning to me, of the curses of intemperance. There was one of the customers at our bar, quite a small boy, who came almost every evening with a little jug, which he had filled with brandy. I never asked the child—but I knew the principal part of his story from his actions. He had a drunken parent! Their dwelling was nigh the tavern. I had occasion, two or three times, to show some little kindness to the boy, when he was rudely treated by the inmates of our place; who exhibited, at times, all those various phases of temper which brandy can produce.

One evening, I had a respite from my employment, and amused myself by my favorite recreation, the theatre. As I was returning quite late, and was passing through a narrow, dirty street, a boy asked me for some pennies, in a piteous tone. He said he wanted them to buy bread. I thought the voice was familiar—and scanning the lad's features, discovered my little acquaintance who had so often brought the jug. Of late, however, I had missed his accustomed visits to the bar. I spoke kindly to him—and the poor fellow, no doubt unaccustomed to such treatment, burst into tears. More and more interested, I inquired of him what distress had sent him forth at that hour; and he acknowledged that, instead of wanting the pennies to buy bread, he wished to purchase liquor—and for his *mother!*

"I don't know what ails her," said the little wretch, "but she acts more strange to-night than I ever saw her before."

"Where does she live?" said I.

"Not a block off," answered the boy. "Wouldn't you just step and see her, sir? She has been ill for a long time."

I thought it no wonder, when, as the child turned to go on before, and show me the way, I caught sight of the little red jug, under his jacket. He led me up a dirty rickety stoop, into a dark entry of the same description; and it was not without considerable risk of my personal safety, that I arrived at last at the door of a room in the attic, where, he said, his mother was lying. He opened the door, and we entered. Never before had I been in so miserable a place. The furniture of the apartment, what there was of it, would have been scouted from a negro hovel. The bed on which the woman herself lay in one corner, was a filthy thing of feathers and soiled rags. Another corner was tenanted by a little girl, the sister of the boy who had conducted me: she was asleep. There was no fire—hardly any light; for the flickering of a half-burned tallow candle on the hearth-stone, only served to cast strange, shadowy hues around, making the place drearier and still more desolate. I stood and looked upon the scene—then, approaching the woman, I gazed down upon her, and, [at] the very first glance I gave in her face, saw that she was dying! Horror-struck, I stepped away from the bed, and for several minutes was silent and motionless with awe.

Every little while, the woman would turn uneasily, and raise herself somewhat from the bed, and look about—oftenest looking at the spot where her girl slumbered. My little guide crouched down close by my feet—it may be that the knowledge of the presence of death was upon him. Again the woman raised herself—then sank wearily back again, her faint groans sounding through the apartment. Poor creature! She was very wretched—and no doubt she had been as guilty as she was wretched; and thoughts of remorse might be the cause of that restlessness which I saw depicted in her countenance. But amid all her agony—amid the dark remembrances that came trooping up there, like fiends in the silence of midnight, to torment her—amid her doubts and fears about the Dim Beyond—amid faintness, and thirstiness, and pain—one controlling thought was mightier than all the rest—motherly love. She called in a hoarse whisper,

"Mary!"

There was no answer. A second time she called, and sank down her head, and held very still, to listen if she was heard. The quiet, regular breathing of the sleeping girl, was the only sound that broke that terrible stillness—for we were mute with dread. Again, the whisper sounded out with even a ghastlier tone than ever before,

"My daughter!"

The hoarse sound seemed to be reëchoed from other voices. It was as if around the room, and peering down from the upper corners of the wall, the death-stricken outcast fancied she saw faces, bodiless, and working with strange grins of mockery. She sat up in the bed—horror giving her strength—and stared wildly about. I was half petrified as her look was directed toward me, and the child at my feet. I stood as still as a statue. With a feeble hand, she drew from its place, the rag-heap used for her pillow; she tightened and bound it with her trembling fingers—I looking on in wonder the while—and then she threw it toward *me!* I half shrieked with fear.

The woman was plainly losing her senses, as the dread moment came nigh.

"Oh, Jack!" she exclaimed, as she saw her boy near me, "come to your poor mother!"

I raised the child, and bade him obey her. He was frightened at her fearful wildness, and crept toward the bed with trembling steps.

"Dear one, lean to my face!" she said.

The poor lad speechlessly obeyed the injunction. The girl slept on. And now the dying woman lay, her mouth partly open, drawing in the breath at intervals with a convulsive movement of the jaws. Her face was livid, and covered with large drops of sweat, and her eyes turned upward. It was evident, that she struggled with the Grim Messenger.

To me, the fearful novelty of the scene almost took away all power of speech or action. What I have narrated was done in the space of but few seconds. Indeed, I was not in the room, from first to last, more than ten or twelve minutes. The woman's arm, numb as it was getting to be, wound itself around her child, and pressed him closer. Something like a smile—a most deathly one—settled upon her features. She tried to speak—but just then her sinking powers forbade the effort. It seemed from her looks and faint gestures, that she would have had the boy rouse his sister, and bring her there also. Then she probably felt conscious how very short were her moments, and how she might die ere the drowsy child could be fully awakened. Her pallid lips moved—just moved, and that was all.

"Father in Heaven!" was the slight thin sound, "hallowed be thy name—thy will be done on earth as in heaven—forgive us our trespasses, as——"

A ghastly rattle shook the repentant sinner's neck.

"Forgive us our trespasses——"

There was a choking gush, as of wind and water in the throat.

"Forgive us——"

Her head turned slowly, and fell on its side with a kind of leaden sound; her arm relaxed its hold; and the guilty creature lay there a corpse—her last prayer smothered in its utterance, and her immortal part starting from its now useless tabernacle, to waft itself on the journey for the Strange Land.

# IX

Her image 'tis—to memory dear—
That clings around my heart,
And makes me fondly linger here
Unwilling to depart.
THOMAS WELLS

MORE than two years had now passed away since my leaving the country; and I am coming, reader, to tell of things which nothing but a resolution to relate *all* my adventures, could wring from me. There is a sacredness in some of our sorrows, which prevents them from being fit subjects for the rude and common gaze. Wife of my youth! of my early youth! Forgive me if I transcribe your name, and your worth, for the admiration and example of those who may hear my mention of you!

When I left my bar-keeping duties, for the reasons I have alluded to, I found it necessary to change my residence for a cheaper one. Passing along an upper and quiet street of the city, one day, I noticed a plain, clean-looking house, of wood, with the sign, "Boarding," on the door. I inquired there, and, finding I could be accommodated, soon took up my quarters in it. My fellow-boarders were in the humbler walks of life; but I soon found an attraction which made up for every deficiency.

My landlady was a widow, with only one child, her daughter Mary. She was a modest, delicate, sweet girl, and before I had been in the house a week, I loved her. I do not choose to dwell upon the progress of our affection, for it was mutual. The widow knew nothing of my former intemperance—in fact,

I had desisted, during my residence with her, from any of my dissolute practices.

Six months passed away. I had obtained employment soon after taking up my abode there, in a factory not far from the house; where, though I was forced to labor, and my remuneration was moderate, because I did not understand the business well at first, I was in a fair train for doing better, and getting higher wages. The widow grew sick. She was of the same delicate temperament which her daughter inherited from her, and, in less than a fortnight from the commencement of her illness, she left the world for ever.

Poor Mary! I have seldom seen such violent and inconsolable grief as followed the death of her mother. She leaned on me for support, and no doubt, the deprivation of any other comforter forced her to look to one, who, with all his faults, had a pure passion for her—as the only resource from utter friendliness [friendlessness?].

As soon as it could with propriety be done, after her mother's death, Mary and I were married. And a more happy union never took place; for, possessed of a treasure which no temptation could have induced me to jeopardize, I had quite reformed, and no longer visited my former haunts; while Mary was the most industrious, prudent, and affectionate of young wives. My sweet Mary! ah, even as I write, a tear is almost falling upon the words—for, wicked as I have been, my heart is not callous enough to be unaffected by remembrance of that hapless one. My wife was a *good woman,* if ever God made one. She was not learned or accomplished in the branches that constitute what is called a fashionable education; but she possessed something a million times better than all the abstractions of philosophy, or the ornaments acquired at a genteel boarding-school. She had a gentle, kindly heart; she had good temper; she had an inherent love of truth, which no temptation could seduce aside, and which she never failed to put in practice; she had charity, a disposition to look with an eye of excuse on the faults of her fellow-creatures, and aid them as far as she could in their poverty, and console them in their griefs.

The weeks passed on. We were doing very well for people in our humble circumstances. Debt was unknown to us, at least to any great degree. We never purchased until we saw the means of payment, and never promised unless we had made such arrangements that we felt pretty sure we could perform. I say *we*, for though my wife was a meek woman, I never took any step without consulting over the matter with her; there was no such thing as *my* and *thy*.

But about a year after our marriage, the serpent came into our little Eden! Ambition—the poison that rankles in the hearts of men, and scorches all peace, and blights the bloom of content—ambition entered there. What is called low life, affords, perhaps, as much scope for this intoxicating passion, as that sphere which called forth the ardor of Napoleon, or which brings into play the mighty minds of statesmen. And petty as the objects among the poor may seem, they are striven for as eagerly, and the chase after them is attended with as many doubts, and as many fluctuations and fevers, as mark the gaining of generalships or cabinet offices.

One of the proprietors at the factory where I was employed owned some vacant lots, in a rather pleasant part of the city, one of which he proposed I should purchase from him. Straightway visions of independence and a home of my own, and the station of a man of property, floated before my eyes. I accepted the offer, and as the terms were very favorable, I for a time found no inconvenience from my new purchase. Not long afterward, I thought I had a good opportunity of hiring money enough to put up a convenient house upon my lot—and I took advantage of the opportunity. As ill-luck, and partly my own ill-judgment, would have it, when the house was about half finished, my means fell out, and I could not go on with the work. We pondered, my wife and I, and we worried, and turned a great many projects in our minds—but none were able to be put in effect. At this stage my creditors grew alarmed, and demanded what was due them. Had it been to save my life, I could not raise the money. They were inexorable—and at one fell swoop all my towering dreams of happiness and a competency were crushed to the dust, by their seizing on my little property, and putting it to a forced sale. The house, unfinished as it was, did not bring one quarter what I had expended upon it. I was half crazed with mortification and disappointment.

Yet—yet we might have been happy. Yet we might have risen, and baffled our evil genius—yet we might have gained our little place back again, in time—and, wiser by experience, kept our wishes within moderate bounds, and journeyed on pleasantly until our appointed number of years had been fulfilled. But the Great Master, in his unfathomable wisdom, allowed it not to be so. For comfort in my sorrows, I frequented my old places of resort, the drinking-shops, and the bar-rooms: I bent beneath the storm, and went back to habits which, until then, my poor Mary had never even suspected as belonging to me.

How well do I remember the first night I returned home, and showed my wife that she had bound her fortunes to a *drunkard!* She had been sitting up for me, for many weary hours, until midnight passed away, and exhausted nature could stand it no longer. She sank her head on the table by her side, and slept. The noise of my shutting the street door awakened her, and she sprang to receive me, and inquire the cause of my absence. Alas! the light she carried in her hand showed her too plainly the bitter reason of that absence—the terrible truth that I was intoxicated! Steeped as my senses were in liquor, I was alarmed at her sudden paleness, and the sickly look which spread over her features. She almost fell to the ground—so agonized were her feelings.

The fatal habit once taken up again, seemed to revive with even more than its former strength and violence. I disregarded my business; and, before long, grew so heedless of my wife's comforts, that I neglected to provide even those matters which are indispensable to subsistence. Where was my former love? Where the old tenderness, and the vow I had made to love and protect? Ah, reader! intemperance destroys even the remembrance of love—and this is one of the most horrible of its consequences. To think that the affection of the early years—the kind and innocent tenderness, which was reciprocated from heart to heart, and which was as a fountain of fond joy—to think all this is given up, merely for a beastly and gross appetite, is painful and fearful indeed!

I sicken as I narrate this part of my story. The recollection comes of the sufferings of my poor wife, and of my unkindness to her. I paid no attention to her comforts, and took no thought for her subsistence. I *think* I never proceeded to any act of violence—but God only knows what words I spoke in my paroxysms of drunken irritation, to that humble, uncomplaining creature. Yes; I remember well, with what agony she has often leaned over my prostrate form, and the hot tears that fell upon my bloated face. I remember the gathering degradation that fixed itself round our name. I remember how my wretched Mary's face grew paler and paler every day—the silent uncomplaining method of her long, long time of dying—for my conduct killed her at last. I remember the scorn and jeers of unfeeling neighbors—the avoidance of me by my old friends—the sinking, grade by grade, until it was at length as though there were no lower depths in which to sink—all are burnt into my mind, Oh, how ineffaceably!

Then came the closing scene of that act of the tragedy. My wife, stricken to the heart, and unable to bear up longer against the accumulating weight of shame and misery, sank into the grave—the innocent victim of another's drunkenness. Oh, that solemn—that terribly solemn hour of her death! Thank God! I was sober at the time—and received her forgiveness. I did not weep as she died, for my throat and the fountains of my eyes, were alike parched and dry. I rushed madly from the house—I knew not and cared not whither. Hell seemed raging in my breast. All my cruelty—all my former love—all my guilt—all my disregard of the sacred ties—seemed concentrated in a thought, and that thought pressing like a mountain of fire all round my heart.

It was night. I walked madly and swiftly through the streets, and though the people stared, I recked not of their notice, but kept my way. What would I have given for power to call back but one little year? One moment only, did I think of drowning my horrible agony in drink; but I cursed the very reflection, as it was formed in my soul. Now, I thought upon Mary's tenderness to me—upon her constant care, and regard, and love; and now, the idea of the repayment I had made her, filled my bosom.

As I wended thus heedlessly on with long strides, I came off against the entrance of a tavern which, in times past, I had frequently visited. In the door, talking with a party of companions, stood a form which, in the imperfect light, I thought I recognized. Another moment, he turned, and his face was shone upon by the gas-lamp; I was right in my conjecture—It was Colby. With a sudden revulsion of feeling, I remembered that it was he who had tempted me, and through whose means all my follies and crimes had been committed. I sprang madly toward the place where he stood.

"Devil!" cried I furiously, seizing him by the throat, "you have brought death to one for whom I would willingly have suffered torments for ever! It is fitting that you pay the penalty with your own base life. Die! villain, even on the spot where you started me upon *my* ruin!"

I clutched him with a grasp of desperation. Those who stood near, were motionless with amazement and fright—and in two minutes more, I had added *murder* to my other crimes. Happily for both, myself and the one I would have made my victim—as he had made me his—the bystanders recovered their self-possession sufficiently soon to interfere, and prevent the accomplishment of my sanguinary purpose. They dragged me from his neck, and relieved him from the imminent danger of his situation; for as sure as there is a heaven above, I would have killed that man, had I been left to myself three minutes longer.

# X

> Dehortations from the use of strong liquors have been the favorite topic of declaimers in all ages, and have been received with abundance of applause by water-drinking critics. But with the patient himself, the man that is to be cured, unfortunately their sound has seldom prevailed. Yet the evil is acknowledged—the remedy simple. Abstain. No force can oblige a man to raise the glass to his head against his will. 'Tis as easy as not to steal—not to tell lies.
>
> CHARLES LAMB

DURING the days that followed, one thought alone—apart from my engrossing grief and remorse—possessed my mind. It was a desire to leave the city, where I had come merely to go astray from the path of honor and happiness, and find relief for my sorrow in a new place, and amid the faces of strangers. It may easily be supposed, that after what I have described in the last chapter, I felt no desire to continue in my course of dissipation. Whether my good resolves held out for any length of time, will be seen in the sequel. I had my household effects sold, and gathering in several debts that were due me, I found I had quite a respectable sum of cash. Careless where I should cast my fortune, so that I got away from New York, I took passage in a steamboat, and journeyed to a small town some thirty miles distant. Here I staid for a few weeks; but getting tired at length of its monotony, I started and went inland, continuing my travel for a day and a night, and stopping then to rest. I was pleased when I awoke in the morning, with the aspect of the place, and determined to fix my abode there.

I informed the landlord of the hotel of my intentions, and asked him if there was any kind of business upon which I could enter—telling him of the small sum of cash which I had at my disposal. With an appearance of great friendliness, he told me, that he was himself just entering upon some speculations, which were very safe and profitable and which required the assistance of a partner. He told me if I would join with him, I could more than double my money, and that my labors would be very light. The man spoke fair, and his projects seemed plausible. So in the evening, over a bottle of wine, in his own parlor, we sealed our agreement. I found, in truth, that I had but little call upon my services. My leisure I employed in roaming about the surrounding country, and in various country sports.

Though I did not drink to anything like my former excess, I was by no means abstemious. During the afternoon, and frequently when at evening the place was filled with visitors, I indulged myself with wine, and with those drinks, originally derived from our thirsty south—drinks that are very pleasant to the taste, but which have led thousands down the path to the lower stages of intemperance, and at last to ruin. As I did not pay for them when they were used, (the landlord and myself having accounts together) I felt no thought of the expense.

Among my amusements, I have said, were walks about the place. In one of these an incident occurred, where I was the instrument of performing an action that served as some small offset to the much evil I have ever brought, through my weakness of mind, to those about me. Through the village of my residence passed a railroad, and the cars generally stopped there some ten or fifteen minutes. Not far from the depôt was a mill supplied with water from a large pond, along the dam of which, as is usual, were several short sluices, covered with bridges. It was a pleasant place, and the miller, an intelligent countryman, was frequently favored with my visits at his place of labor.

One day, on the arrival of the cars, several of the passengers, being informed that they were to stop a little longer than ordinary, determined to get out, and stroll a few steps for recreation. Among the number was a lady, elegantly dressed, and leading by the hand a little girl, a child of six or seven years. The lady appeared to be very much pleased with the scenery of the pond, and creek; she strolled along the dam, and occasionally stopped to admire some fine prospect, or cull the beautiful pond-flowers which grew upon the banks in great profusion. While she was resting upon one of the narrow bridges I have mentioned, the child scrambled down the banks to pluck a gaudy blossom that had caught her eyes. I was at that moment standing, leaning on the door of the mill, and gazing listlessly at the bustle around the stopping-place of the cars. All of a sudden, there came a loud shriek! The lady was standing upon the dam, the very picture of distraction, and uttering loud and shrill cries for help.

"She will be drowned! For the love of God, come and rescue her!" she cried to me, as, alarmed by her cries, I ran hastily toward the place.

I saw at once what was the matter; the little girl, reaching over after the flower, had lost her balance and fallen into the pond. With promptness, I divested myself of my shoes and coat, and plunged into the pond. Fortunately I was an excellent swimmer. The current was running in from the other side very strongly, and I knew the child must have been carried some distance. I dashed rapidly out, and catching a glimpse of the end of a ribbon, made toward it, and seized the girl, just as she was sinking, probably for the last time. I brought her safely to the shore, and restored her to the arms of her half delirious protector.

Ding-dong! ding-dong! went the bell of the cars, calling the passengers together, and sounding the signal for starting. The lady, carrying the child, hurried toward the depôt, uttering incoherent blessings on my head; and beseeching, if ever I came to New-York, the place of her residence, to call at her house. As she seated herself in the vehicle, she threw me, from the window, a card, with her name, and the street and number of her dwelling, which I placed in my pocket-book. In the very midst of her flood of gratitude, the train rattled away.

As I walked slowly toward the public house where I lived, it may be supposed that my reflections were of a quite complacent nature, for the deed of kindness which I had been performing.

In the course of the ensuing weeks, my want of active employment led me to the glass, as my resource from low spirits. Two or three times I was more than half drunk; and it came to be so, at length, that I could not spend the day as I thought comfortably, without drinking five or six times before dinner, and as many more between that and bedtime. What will the reader think of my resolution of mind? I had made a compact with myself, after my poor Mary's death, that I would drink nothing but wine; and though I stuck to that for a while, I soon caught myself indulging in the stronger kinds of liquor. Perhaps, if I had filled up my time with active employment, I might have kept to my resolution, and even in the end totally reformed. But of what mischief is idleness a parent! That time which hung heavy on my hands, I drowned in the forgetfulness of the oblivion-causing cup.

Reader! perhaps you despise me. Perhaps, if I were by you at this moment, I should behold the curled lip of scorn, and the look of deep contempt. Oh, pause stern reverencer of duty, and have pity for a fellow-creature's weakness! I would ask, with the gentle Elia, that thou shouldst mingle compassion and human allowance with thy disapprobation. With him, too, I say, trample not on the ruins of a man. Thou sayest, perhaps—Begin a reformation, and custom will make it easy. But what if the beginning be dreadful? The first steps, not like climbing a mountain, but going through fire? What if the whole system must undergo a change, violent as that which we conceive of the mutation of form in some insects? What if a process comparable to flaying alive, have to be endured? Is the weakness which sinks under such struggles, to be compared with the pertinacity which clings to vice, for itself and its gross appetites? I have known one (relates the same pleasant moralist I quote above) in that state, when he has tried to abstain but for one evening, though the poisonous potion had long ceased to bring back its first enchantments; though he was sure it would rather deepen his gloom than brighten it, in the violence of the struggle, and the necessity he felt of getting rid of the present sensation at any rate—I have known him to scream out, to cry aloud, for the anguish and pain of the strife within him. Many, perhaps, on whom liquor never produced powerful results will here laugh at a weak brother, who, trying his strength and coming off foiled in the contest, would fain persuade them that such agonistic exercises are dangerous. On them my remarks are wasted. It is to a very different description of persons I speak. It is to the weak—the nervous; to those who feel the want of some artificial aid to raise their spirits in society to what is no more than the ordinary pitch of those around them. Such must fly the convivial class [glass?] in the first instance, if they do not wish to sell themselves, for their term of life, to misery.

A man once, whom I knew well, and whose name was honored over all New-York for his many virtues, was seen by me to take a glass in an obscure drinking-shop. I afterward found that he *had* to drink, or engage in the fearful contest described above. He was of irritable and weak temperament, and though he knew his habits were secretly hurrying him to the grave, he quailed before the agony of the trial. He had commenced it more than once, but was never able to complete his own conquest. Now, though I have an abiding faith in the ability to reform, through the GLORIOUS TEMPERANCE PLEDGE, and the strength which Providence gives to those who honestly set about a good work—yet I know the awful horrors which such men as the one I speak of, must go through. Reader, if you are not one of that sort yourself, you can conceive not of those trials. Not only has habit made liquor necessary to their enjoyment, but to the very action of the vital powers; and at the very time it quickens and brightens their faculties into a dim kind of action, it warns them how it is wafting them onward to the verge of decay with a horrible rapidity!

The pure and virtuous cast scorn upon such as I have been, and as thousands now are. But oh, could they look into the innermost recesses of our hearts, and see what spasms of pain —what impotent attempts to make issue with what appears to be our destiny—what fearful dreams—what ghastly phantoms of worse than hellish imagination—what of all this resides, time and again, in our miserable bosoms—then, I know, that scorn would be changed to pity. It is not well to condemn men for their frailties. Let us rather own our common bond of weakness, and endeavor to fortify each other in good conduct and in true righteousness, which is charity for the errors of our kind. The drunkard, low as he is, is a *man.* The fine capacities, the noble marks which belong to our race, those glorious qualities which the Great Builder stamped upon his masterpiece of works, are with him still. They are not destroyed, but hidden in darkness, as precious gems cast down in the mire. And the object of the truly wise and good will be, to raise him up again; to reform and brighten those capacities, and to set in operation a train of causes, which will afford him a chance of attaining once more a respectable station in society. Once *thoroughly regenerated,* the remembrance of his old defamation will stand before his eyes like a pillar of fire, and warn him back from any further indulgence in his vicious courses.

I am the more particular in my remarks upon this matter, because I have seen so many cases of hopeless and confirmed intemperance, made thus by the injudicious severity of the neighbors and relatives of the unhappy victim. Little aware of the strength of the chains which bind him, and the horrors which surround a man in those moments when he is without that stimulus which custom has rendered necessary to him, they cast every slight upon the drunkard, and are unguarded in their expressions of anger and contempt. A little moderation perhaps, a little friendliness and sympathy, bestowed at the proper moment, would work a complete revolution in his character. But it is not bestowed, and the wretched one goes on from bad to worse, until there is no hope left. I remember a case in point.

While living with my uncle in the country, one of our most esteemed neighbors was a young farmer, lately married, and come with his wife to settle in the town. He had bought a fine little farm, and occasionally when work was pressing, he employed me to assist him, my uncle consenting. During the time I spent in that way, I became acquainted with the circumstances I am going to relate. The name of our neighbor was Fanning.

As was customary in those parts, in the hot days when we were getting in the harvest of hay, and the early grain, a couple of jugs of ardent spirits were brought into the field for the use of the work-people. It has since been a wonder to me that all of the villagers were so tacitly agreed as to the benefit of this custom. Now, medical men, and not only medical men, but all men of common sense know that intoxicating drinks are highly detrimental to the strength, and improper for use during laborious employment. They sap the very essence of energy, and prostrate the arm of the strong man. A feverish impulse may be given for a moment; but it reacts in a tenfold deficiency of power for twenty times as long a time. Be that as true as it undoubtedly is, however, among Fanning and his fellow-townsmen it was the common custom.

Fanning had a brother, a middle-aged, gentlemanly man, who possessed a small estate, invested in stocks, from whence he drew a moderate stipend. A portion of the year he was employed in a village near by as a school teacher.

I knew the man, and loved him well. He was a quiet, good natured person, and wherever he went, he made friends. I recollect his looks, too, and some little peculiarities he had. He was small in figure, with bright black eyes and very long fine glossy hair, which used to fall quite down upon his shoulders. Notwithstanding the modest disposition of "the little teacher," as the people used to call him, his laugh and his voice was loud among the loudest, at the merry-makings in the neighborhood, which he invariably attended. He wore a round jacket always, which was one of his peculiarities. His size and his juvenile method of apparel, made him look like anything but a pedagogue.

The teacher, when he was not employed in his profession, would frequently aid his brother, in the work of the farm. He used to come into the field, in hay time, and give his assistance there. We always welcomed him, for his pleasant mirth cast a charm on all around.

"Mr. Fanning," said one of the men, one day, "if you work with us, you should do as we do. The jug has passed round, and every person drinks but yourself."

"Is it needful, then," said the teacher, laughing, "that I partake of the liquor, in order to be on even-footing with the rest?"

"Of course," was the general rejoinder; "of course."

"Well, then," said Fanning, "here goes."

And he took down a moderate draught.

The whole conversation was intended as a mere joke, of course—such light talk as work-people amuse themselves with during the intermission between their morning and afternoon labors. But it proved in the end, a fatal joke to the poor teacher.

The next day, the same bantering was passed, and Fanning drank again. It is hardly necessary that I should narrate the particulars of the method by which he became a lover of the liquid that at first he regarded with such apathy. It was all, however, plainly to be traced to the accidental invitation given him in the harvest-field. Before the end of the summer, he could drink his two or three glasses with great satisfaction, and even became an habitual visitor at the bar-room.

I have noted down thus minutely the incident which led to the teacher's intemperance, because I think it by no means an isolated case. There are many, no doubt, who will get this book, who may be the witnesses, and even practisers, of a habit of having liquor in the fields during the hot farm-work of the summer. For this lamentable habit, contrary as it is to the dictates of prudence and common sense, is not an altogether exploded one.

The teacher, as I have said, grew to the desire for drink. He conducted his school that winter, as usual, though before the end of the session, he had more than one fit of intoxication.

Summer came again. The pernicious jugs were brought into the field, and the elder Fanning was their best customer. Hardly a week passed without his being completely steeped two or three times in drunkenness. I have myself seen him lying beside the hay-cocks, divested of sense and rationality, more like a brute than a human being. He had always been attached to me, and would frequently obey my persuasions to go home, or to desist from any further indulgence in liquor, when, to any one else, he was abusive and obstinate.

"Frank!" said he to me one day, when he was just sobered from a spree, "I am a very wicked and foolish man—if things go on in this way, what is to become of me?"

I made no answer, though I was highly pleased at hearing him talk thus.

"Yes," he continued, "it certainly will not do. I cannot—I *will not* allow myself to become a common drunkard. The thought is horrible!"

A good resolution, once formed, may be broken, it is true; but the very process of reflection which leads to the forming of the resolution, is favorable to improvement. If brought back often to such reflections, it is twenty to one but the improvement will be effectual at last.

We had been sitting together, the teacher and I, in his apartment, as he made the remarks I have quoted above. We rose and went down to the common sitting-room, where Mrs. Fanning was engaged in some domestic employments.

"Is my brother home?" asked the teacher.

The woman made no reply, and Fanning repeated the question.

"If he is," was the answer, with a sneer, "it's not likely he cares about seeing a drunken sot!"

The teacher said nothing, but sat down upon a chair near the window. Soon after the farmer came in, but took no notice of the now sobered inebriate. He brushed through the room with a haughty glance, as much as to say, I feel no wish to be familiar with such as thou.

I was standing in the door, just about to depart, and my feelings could not help sympathizing with my poor friend, thus scorned by those who were nearest and dearest to him. True, he had acted wrongly, but they need not have thus wounded him in so unprovoked a manner. He rose from his chair, and we walked forth together. I could see that he felt very much agitated. As I diverged from the road to go my own way, I prayed Heaven to continue in his soul the sentiments he had a few moments before expressed to me.

Without doubt, had he not been treated thus scornfully by his brother and sister-in-law, the reflections of the teacher would have led to his becoming a temperate man. But in his lonesomeness and weariness of heart, he retreated to the bar-room. He drank deeply, and that night saw him in a more severe intoxication than ever before. Provoked very much at his conduct, the farmer and his young wife would hardly use him with ordinary decency. It was only the odium of having him taken up as a common vagrant, that prevented their turning him entirely out of doors.

"Oh!" he has many a time said to me, "if there were only some little fastening of good-will among my family, where I could cast anchor, I feel assured I might be saved yet. But I am maddened by the coldness and contempt of my brother and his wife, when I am in a fit state to feel it. It is more poignant than even the pangs which are a result of my drinking!"

Twenty times, in his lucid intervals, did he express this opinion to me. I have no doubt it came from his very heart.

And now, all his friends dropped off from him. He was considered by them, I suppose, as a disgrace to their name. They would cross the street to avoid meeting him; they would forbid his entrance to their houses; and every contumely was heaped upon him. Of course, he could obtain his old employment of teacher no more; and the children, who formerly loved and respected him, now looked upon him with disgust. This, he told me, was one of the bitterest of his punishments.

I solemnly believe that even yet, degraded as he was, he might have been reformed, by his friends seizing a lucky moment, and by their treating him as a fellow-creature, instead of a beast. But they did not so. His frailties were visited by their virulence; and they forgot entirely that common bond of fellowship which, as we all sin more or less, should have caused them to be lenient. Which of those friends or relatives can say—I have, on my conscience, none of the responsibility of that man's intemperance and death?

The teacher was of naturally delicate constitution, and he could not long hold up under the results of his conduct. Each successive indulgence left him a weaker and a weaker man.

Three years had not passed away, after his taking that draught from the jug in the harvest-field, before he was upon his dying bed—the dying bed of a drunkard. With his last breath he proclaimed that his wretched fate might have been prevented, had not the thoughts of reformation, whenever they arose in his mind, been stifled by the proud and contemptuous treatment he received from his relatives and friends.

# XI

*Whene'er thou meet'st a human form*
*Less favor'd than thine own,*
*Remember, 'tis thy neighbor worm,*
*Thy brother, or thy son.*

ANONYMOUS

WHEN I had been some five months in this village, I thought one morning that it would not be amiss for me to have a settlement with the landlord. Since the time I had confided my funds to him, I had heard very little of our joint speculations; and I supposed I might have quite a handsome amount of cash due me by this time.

Upon my mentioning the subject, he assented at once—stating that he had for a day or two intended suggesting the same thing to me. We therefore went into his little private parlor, and he drew out his books, and commenced reckoning. What was my amazement when he informed me that the amount due *from me to him* was not quite one hundred dollars! I supposed at first he was in a vein of pleasantry, and laughed at him. But he gravely pushed his accounts over to me, and told me to look for myself. Considerably alarmed, I did so. I saw that one single item, that of *liquor* alone, was summed up to more than the sum I had orginally put in his hands, for purposes of profit. I indignantly asked him if he thought I was going to submit to such flagrant injustice. With an impudent coolness, he retorted that if I chose to attempt redress, I might begin as soon as I thought fit. Had he not been liberal, he said, his demand against me would have been much higher.

The man was a rascal—that was evident. But whether I had

any chance of recovering back my money was not quite so clear. Upon consulting with a man of law, in the course of the day, I found that my prospect was gloomy indeed. I have since thought, that the landlord himself gave the lawyer his cue. Quite mad with resentment and agitation, when I returned to the house, I told the landlord plainly my opinion of his conduct. He retorted. My temper rose, and I struck him to the earth. I rushed from the house, swearing that I would not stay in so vile a place another night.

I had a small sum of money, and I immediately engaged passage to New York. In an hour I was on my way thither. The reflections that filled my mind, were anything but agreeable. To be swindled—to be the dupe of a villain, and one too whom I had looked on as a friend—was bad enough. Besides which, I could not but be conscious how much I was to blame for my own carelessness, and my want of sobriety, which, after all, was the foundation of the ill-luck.

The latter part of my journey was by steamboat. As the light of day dawned in the east, our craft swung alongside the wharf; and I went on shore in the city, where, four years previous, I had come an innocent and honest country youth. My unsophisticated habits had worn away, but at the expense of how much of the pure gold, which was bartered for dross!

Of course, I had no plan marked out as to any method of life, or any means to get a living. As I walked along the street, but a few rods from the landing-place, my eyes were caught by the sight of tempting bottles of liquor, arranged on a bar. What busy devil was it that tempted me then to go in and drink? Yielding to the fatal impulse, I entered and called for liquor. The ice was broken now, and I felt no more repugnance. There were some jovial-looking fellows there, and I entered into conversation with them. A little while, and we all drank again.

From that moment, I have an indistinct recollection of going through scenes which it makes my stomach now turn, to think upon—drunkenness, and the very lowest and filthiest kind of debauchery. Probably, for I never knew for certain, I spent five days upon that spree. Not at any single time was I sober, or near sober.

At last I awoke. It was a little before sunrise. I lay upon the ground, on a pier jutting out into the river. By one side of me was a high pile of wood—on the other side I heard the dashing of water against the wharf. The air, though chill, was fresh and fragrant; but the torments of the damned seemed raging in my head. Oh, that agony of pain; that thirstiness; that searing, burning dryness; that indescribable feeling of horror; that detestable nausea—never shall I forget!

I raised myself on my hands and knees, and my first thought was to throw myself over into the river, and thus put an end to my miserable existence. But, wicked as I was, I dared not rush thus blindly into the presence of an offended God. I lifted myself, and sat on the heavy piece of timber that formed the edge of the wharf.

What a miserable object! The thing I wore upon my head was crushed out of all shape of a hat; my trowsers were torn and soiled; I had no coat, and but one shoe. My face, I felt, was all dirty and brown, and my eyes bleared and swollen. What use had I for life? While, at the moment, I feared to die. And as it seemed that even now I felt the icy finger at my heart—I prayed to God that he would not crush the wounded worm.

I arose, and walked forth.

The hours rolled on. The streets filled with clatter and with busy faces; and wherever I passed along, the crowd shrunk from me as from the pestilence.

I remember that about noon I came out into Chatham Square. On one side were little hills of furniture of every description and quality. Many people were scanning them, apparently with the intent to become purchasers. There were also auctioneers, mounted upon tables, or barrels, and crying the goods and the prices that were bid for them. Toward the middle of the Square stood a row of coaches, and several carts, for hire. On the walks, and through the streets, hundreds of men, women, and children were constantly passing, crowd upon crowd. I stood awhile, and looked upon the scene, though vacantly.

Then I sauntered on again. All around was the deafening noise of people engaged in their thousand employments. I gazed curiously at the shops, which exhibited their merchandise in large handsome windows, many of them having a few of their best articles hung out in front, so that the passer-by could not but see them. After awhile, I turned and went up a cross street. So on I wended, and across, and up and down, like a rudderless boat.

Dragging thus about, four or five hours passed away, and I began to grow foot-sore and very hungry.

Signs now appeared of the coming on of night. Lamplighters hurried past me with their ladders; the windows, one after another, began to touch up their gas; and those of the mechanics whose business was earliest through, were to be seen in groups, walking along homeward. As I came out from a narrow street, through which I had been wandering some time, I found myself in the same open place, where at noon I had seen such busy traffic. What could I do? I cast my eyes hopelessly about, and saw no sign of sunshine. I felt quite faint from want of food.

There seemed to be no better plan than to walk down the wide handsome street, leading to the east from where I stood, and knock at every house, stating my destitute situation, and asking for the remnants of a meal, and shelter or the means of shelter, until I should obtain relief. Beggary! It was a bitter pill, but I saw no medium between it and starvation; and at the best, the chances were ten to one that I should not gain what I sought.

I walked along the street. It was lined on each side with lofty brick houses. There was no flash of shop windows, and much less noise, and fewer passengers than in the thoroughfares I had hitherto seen.

As I wearily trod the flag-stones, my eyes would now and then be caught by the front rooms of the basements, some of them with family groups circling round the cheerful fire, some with the table spread for supper, and with many luxuries and comforts to tempt the appetite. Oh, how my mouth watered! Here and there I beheld through the curtains little children, all fresh and neat, and curled, frolicking about in play.

It was a long time before I could screw my courage to make application at the doors. At last I went up the stoop of one of the houses, and knocked softly with my fist. I waited several minutes, and then knocked again; no one came to open for me, and I was about retreating in despair.

"Pull the bell, my man," said a person passing, who noticed my conduct, "they'll never hear your knock."

So I applied my hand to the knob, and drew it just enough to make a slight tinkle. In a few minutes, a black man came, and swinging the door on its hinges, beheld me standing there, abashed and trembling.

"Well, what is it?" said he, after waiting a moment, and hearing me say nothing.

I began my request, but had not spoken more than four or five words, before the menial slammed the door in my face with an execration. Starting like a guilty creature, I hastily rushed down upon the walk again.

I passed several blocks before making another attempt. This time I applied at the lower entrance. A woman appeared to answer the summons.

"Come in," she answered compassionately, "wait a bit, and I'll speak to the mistress."

She went in through a side door, and I could hear talking in the apartment. After a short time the door partly opened.

"No," said some one within, "imposters are so common, and you only encourage them in idleness. Tell him to go; and be careful of the bolt, when he passes out."

The woman came from the room, and her face told the cheerless answer, she was commissioned to bear, without the necessity for words. The next minute I was in the dark street once more.

A third and fourth trial were as fruitless as the first.

At the next, the servant told me to wait awhile, as the family were at their devotions. I stood, and gazed at the circle in the inner apartment; for the door was open, and I could see all. An elderly gentleman was reading a portion of Scripture, and the rest were listening with sedate attention to all that came from his lips.

*"Inasmuch,"* I heard him say, in a slow emphatic voice, his eyes fixed reverently on the book before him; *"Inasmuch as ye have refused it to the least of these my brethren, ye have refused it to me."*

More he read of the same purport—and then closed the book and knelt, the rest following his example.

For fifteen minutes, nothing was heard there but the accents of fervent prayer. Then all arose, and after a decorous pause, the servant introduced my case. He was sufficiently bred to his station, to refrain from urging my claims in any other way than a statement of my destitute condition; yet I could not have had a more favorable advocate. When he finished,

"Richard," said the elderly gentleman, "give the poor fellow this."

The servant took the gift, and put it in my hand. It was *one cent.*

And Richard hurried me out of the light; for he felt his

face suffused with a blush. And as I was leaving the door, he unclasped my finger and placed there a silver coin, just twenty-five times the value of what his master had bestowed upon me.

For my life I could not have subjected myself to any more rebuffs. I remembered a low groggery, where cheap lodgings were to let, and turned my wretched steps toward the place.

# XII

*What brings vice and guilt below?*
*Strong drink brings!*

TEMPERANCE SONG

MONTHS swept onward in their silent course. I know not how I lived; I have never been able, to this day, to account for the method of my subsistence—but yet I did live. Sometimes, finding a chance shelter in a half finished building, left open by the workmen—sometimes, sleeping in the purlieus of the markets, or on the docks—sometimes, going for two days with hardly a morsel of food, for I was a drunkard still; and though necessity at times made me sober for a while, I always managed to get liquor by one means or another, at last. Can it be believed that, at the very moment the eyes of the reader are scanning these pages, there are hundreds—ay thousands—roaming about the by-places of this mighty city, in the same condition, and with the same appetite, which I have described as mine during those fearful months? It seems now, as I look back to it, like a dream—a hideous phantom of a diseased mind. But there came a sudden shock after a time, and I was aroused from that mockery of a dream. Thus it came.

It was the midnight of a Sabbath in winter. Darkness spread over the great city, and the slumbering dwellers therein. The streets, the mighty veins along which currents had coursed all day, were now still and deserted. Every hour the booming of the public clocks pealed out, each stroke falling distinctly and solemnly through the frosty night air. Overhead, the stars did not shine. It had been snowing, and the wind occasionally blew the drifts so as to make a perfect tempest of fine ice, dashing into the face of the late traveller. The drowsy watchman sought some sheltered nook, and drew himself close together, shivering with the rigor of the night.

Starting at one of the eastern wharves, is a street running up from the river—a narrow, dirty street, with many wooden houses, occupied as taverns for seamen and abiding places for degraded women. At one of these taverns, myself, and a party of ill-favored, gallows-looking fellows, were arranging our persons, preparatory to sallying forth in the streets. What object could we have in view, at that late hour of the night, but wickedness?

There were four of us. The leader of our gang, who was addressed by the name of Picaroon, had several weapons about his person that were evidently capable of doing dangerous work.

"Come lads," said he, "the business we are on, will be none the worse for a few glasses. Let us drink."

At the word, we helped ourselves, and tossed the liquor down our throats.

We made our egress from the place, and sticking our hands in the capacious pockets of our coats, we walked rapidly after the Picaroon, who strode ahead, as if he knew at once the road to be taken.

The wind whistled, and the fitful blasts, laden with the drift-snow, assailed our progress, and dashed in our faces as we walked along. But our leader turned neither to the right or left, and hardly deigned to bend his head to the heaviest demonstrations of the tempest.

After awhile we reached a section of the city, mostly occupied by merchants for their warehouses and stores. The Picaroon now proceeded more cautiously, and turning up Wall-street, led us to a place, not far distant from the Exchange, where we stopped—partly to take breath, and partly to reconnoitre. The night was so dark that a man at a rod's distance could not have been seen. So we listened awhile, to hear if any of the guardians of the hour were stirring.

"I believe," said the Picaroon, in a low tone, "that we are on the right track. This, I think, is the place we seek."

And he pointed to a basement immediately in front of us, which from its appearance, and the sign over the door, looked like a broker's office.

"Now boys," continued our conductor, in the same cautious voice, "let us begin. Banks, where is the key I gave you in charge?"

The person he addressed handed it to him in silence.

"Curses!" exclaimed the Picaroon, vainly trying to put it to successful use, "the thing has failed, after all. I more than suspected it would. The next time, I'll take the duplicate myself."

"Then we'll burst open the door," said one of our party.

"Of course," the Picaroon rejoined, "we have nothing else to do. Here Evans, hold this lantern!"

And coming up at his orders, I took the light, which was shaded on all sides but one, and held it as he directed.

They proceeded to their work of crime. *They?* Why should I not say *we?* For though a passive agent in the affair, I stood by with apathetic consent, and aided in it. Sunk, sunk at last, to be the companion and abettor of thieves!

"D—n the door! how firm it is!" said Banks, as his cautious blows with a sort of crow-bar, produced no effect. The Picaroon had previously used two or three saws, and was now at work with a chisel.

Our other companion was assisting actively, also, and I stood, and threw the rays from the lantern as they desired.

Crash! crash! went the instruments of our burglary, with a deadened sound, for we knew there were private watchmen in this part of the city—and though we feared little from their vigilance such a night as that, we thought our blows, if too loud, might reach their ears, and bring on a discovery.

Yielding, at last, to saw-teeth, chisel-edge, and crow-bar, the fastenings gave way. One stout thump with the latter instrument, and our entrance was clear. But it was louder than any of the preceding ones.

"Hell!" muttered the Picaroon, furiously, "I would rather have worked two hours longer than heard that blow! But it is too late now; so, Banks, come in with me, and you two keep watch here!"

He had hardly stepped out of sight, when a watchman's rattle rang on the curb-stone, not a hundred feet from where we stood. The Picaroon and his companions heard it too, and dashing from the door, threw the lantern on the ground, and fled along the street.

"Quick! quick! for your lives!" cried the Picaroon to us as he passed. "Both of you, run for your lives!"

My companion took advantage of the timely warning; but the watch were now upon our steps. I heard them close behind me, and stumbling in the darkness, fell upon the ground. They seized me, and carried me away a prisoner. The whole occurrence passed over like a whirlwind. Neither of my three companions were taken.

Was I not sunk low indeed? The very stupor, the deadened nature of my faculties—even when not under the influence of liquor which my course of life had super-induced—was not sufficient to hide from me the horrible feature of my situation. A criminal, one who had violated the laws, and was justly obnoxious to their severest punishments—where could I look for a friend, or whence hope for favor?

It were a stale homily, were I to stay here, and remark upon the easy road from intemperance to crime. Those who have investigated those matters, tell us, however, that five out of every six of the cases which our criminal courts have brought before them for adjudication, are to be traced directly or indirectly to that fearful habit. I have sometimes thought, that the laws ought not to punish those actions of evil which are committed when the senses are steeped in intoxication. But if such a principle were allowed to influence judicial decisions, how terrible an opening there would be! How great a temptation, even, to the letting loose of the worst passions! An idiot is not responsible for his actions, to be sure; but the drunkard deliberately brings his idiocy upon himself, and must not take shelter under it from the consequences thereof. And yet, that mercy and charity which should ever be present in our minds, must lead us to throw the mantle of excuse, as far as possible, over the bad done by the intemperate. None know —none can know, but they who have felt it—the burning, withering thirst for drink, which habit forms in the appetite of the wretched victim of intoxication.

# XIII

*Be free! not chiefly from the iron chain,*
*But from the one which passion forges, be*
*The master of thyself!*

MRS. EMBURY

WHEN I was turning over in my mind, the second day of my confinement in prison, the method I had best pursue, under all my present difficulties, the darkest and fearfullest despondency fell upon me. It seemed like a cloud stretching all around and over me, and hiding every glimpse of the cheerful light. The thought of my boyhood in the country—of a hundred different scenes in the happy life I had spent there—came to my remembrance. Then my journey to New York, and my companions of the market-wagon. The antiquary, Lee, my benefactor, to whom I had made so poor a return, and Colby, the instrument of my disgrace. I pondered upon all, and even the minutest incidents of that journey. Lee! Should I not apply to him in my tribulation? But no; I had injured him deeply, and my pride revolted at the idea of his knowing my present situation. And as for Colby, since the death of my poor wife, and our rencontre at the tavern, I would as soon have taken a serpent in my hand as received a favor from him.

The despondency I have mentioned, clung to me for days. I, a young man, on whom fortune had more than once smiled, whose very start of life in the city was signalized by a stroke of good luck, that might have led me on to a competence and happiness; and here I was, imprisoned for a heinous crime. More than once the fiendish resolve entered my mind, of foul self-murder! But ever the image of my sainted Mary came to me in those prison walls, and looked down, and smiled pleasantly; and I could not renounce all hope of ever seeing her again, by sealing up the sum of my wickedness beyond all power of pardon.

The time approached for my trial. So callous was I, and so resigned to my fate, that I cared little whether it went well or ill for me.

A day or two before I was to be brought up in court, one of the officers of the prison entered, stating that a gentleman without desired to see me; and he had hardly spoken the words, when the person in question was ushered into my cell. He was a middle-aged man, and what he could wish with me I could not conceive.

"Is your name Franklin Evans?" said he.

I answered in the affirmative.

"Do you know that card?"

And he handed me a dirty piece of pasteboard, with a name written upon it. The name was *"Lucy Marchion*—Bleecker-street."

Surprised at the question, and utterly unconscious of what the man's conduct could mean, I made no answer, but stared at him in surprise.

"Listen," continued he. "The lady, whose name you hold in your hand, was many months since at a distant place in the country, with a dear child. Accidentally the child fell into a dangerous stream of water, and would have been drowned, but for the kindness of a brave young stranger, who rescued it, and restored it to the lady. She was hurried away, almost on the instant, leaving in that stranger's hand, her name and residence. By some mark upon the card, the whole circumstance was brought to her mind this very morning, when a police officer called, and handed it to us, making inquiries, which it is unnecessary here to repeat."

The man ceased; and I knew the whole affair intuitively. In a preceding chapter I have mentioned the incident, where I preserved the little girl's life. The card I had placed in my pocket-book, never thinking of it since. Upon the morning after my arrest, my person had been searched, and everything taken from me—the authorities thinking, that perhaps some clue might be gained to my accomplices. The card, they fancied, could possibly afford some such clue. They went to the address upon it. Mr. Marchion, the husband of the lady, and the father of the little girl I had preserved, was a lawyer, well known for his talent and respectability; and, at the solicitation of his wife, he immediately started upon a mission of benevolence to the prison where I was.

"Tell me, young man," said he, when all this was fairly understood between us, and he knew that he had indeed found the person for whom his wife had never ceased to pray down blessings—"tell me the whole story of your crime, for which you are now in durance. Keep back nothing; and I will see what can be done for you."

"Is there any prospect," inquired I, anxiously, "for acquittal, think you?"

"That question I can best answer," said he, "after your story is told."

I knew that I could place implicit reliance upon his honor, and I related the whole incidents of my folly and my crime. I told him, that for weeks my faculties had been drowned amid a sea of intemperance. I said that when I started off with the Picaroon and the others, I knew not where they were going, or for what purpose; and that, though I stood by, I had no hand in the active commission of the burglary. My defence, I could not help seeing myself, was a very weak one; but it was the best I had to offer, and the love of liberty was strong within me.

"Perhaps it would be wiser," said Mr. Marchion, when I concluded, "for me to express no opinion now; and yet I would advise you not to give up hope. The judge, whom I know well, is one that will not be apt to look upon your conduct, placed in the light you have given to it by the narrative just closed, with a too rigorous eye; and I feel assured that what you have spoken is the truth."

And as he departed, I felt new cheerfulness spring up in my breast. So pleasant is it, in time of dismay, to have one good heart, on whose friendly aid you can rest your troubles.

Before the trial, Mr. Marchion came to me two or three times again, to get the locality of the tavern whence we had started, on the night of the burglary. He also took from me the names of two or three persons, whom I had known in my better days, for witnesses that I had once borne a fair reputation. I felt some doubt, as I gave him that of Mr. Lee, among others, whether the character my old friend might give me, would prove to my advantage or no.

The crisis came at last. The prosecuting attorney proved by the officers the fact of the crime, beyond the possibility of cavil. The officers swore, also, that, according to all appearance, I was one of the robbers. They had arrested me on the spot, in a vain endeavor to fly.

Mr. Marchion himself conducted my defence. He skillfully enlarged on the danger of circumstantial evidence—produced his witnesses to my former good name and honorable conduct —and then expatiated on the unhappy method of my having fallen into habits of intemperance. The keeper of the low tavern proved my evident ignorance, when the Picaroon led me away, of the business on which he was bound; and with all the dexterity for which his profession is celebrated, my fervent advocate dressed up what good points there were in my case, and closed by a pathetic appeal jointly to the jury and the court.

All was of no avail. The jury, after being out an hour or two, came in with a verdict of *"Guilty."* I could hardly support myself under the sickening sensation which followed the utterance of that word. My head swam, my ears tingled, and I heard not the foreman continue, "and recommended to the mercy of the court." Had I done so, I should hardly have hoped for any leniency—so sure had I been, after Mr. Marchion's eloquent appeal, that I must be acquitted.

The judge consulted with those on each side of him for a

few minutes, and then rose to pronounce sentence. I could hardly believe my ears, when they conveyed to me, as he went on, the intelligence that I was *not* to be sent back to prison. Amazed and overjoyed, I noted but little of the details of his discourse: how that in view of the peculiar nature of my case, sentence was to be suspended, and I discharged—or something of that sort. I only heard the word *discharged*, and could hardly remain in the box until he finished his speech. Then, as the officer in attendance came to me, and took me by the hand, and told me I was free, I rushed aside, and caught Mr. Marchion's arm, which I dampened with my tears. *Free!* Yes, after all—after being on the very verge of punishment for felony—to come off thus! Was it not, indeed, a fit cause for rejoicing?

# XIV

*Kneel! and the vow thou breathest there*
*At that lone hour shall float on high;*
*Spirits of light shall bless thy prayer,*
*The dead, the crowned, shall greet thy sigh.*

MRS. HALE'S MAGAZINE

THE kindness of Marchion and his wife did not pause merely at saving me from an ignominious fate. I pass over the gratitude of the lady at our first meeting, the very next hour after I was liberated from bondage—simply stating, that it was fully such as a mother might be supposed to offer one who had saved her offspring from sudden and painful death.

"All that we could do," said the lady, "would not pay you, generous man, for the service you have rendered me."

And she called the little girl to her side, and bade her thank the preserver of her life. Marchion stood by, and looked on with a friendly smile.

But stop—thought I to myself, my eyes being caught by the sight of my own soiled and tattered garments—am I a fit person for the company of well-dressed and cleanly people? What excuse should I make? But Marchion already knew a large part of my history, and of my former follies; and some good spirit seemed whispering to me, no excuse but the truth. So in answer to their inquiries, I told them my whole life, without any alteration or concealment.

"Young man," said the lady, when I ended, "had you related all this to us some months ago, we should have shrunk from you, or set you down as a liar. But my observation, of late, has led both my husband and myself to the knowledge of cases, exceeding even yours in wonder and in depth of misery."

She then told me that her husband, who had in his younger

days been an intemperate man, was now a member of one of the societies of the city, whose object was to aid the holy cause of Abstinence; and that at the meetings of those societies, which she occasionally attended, she had heard in the "experience," of those who addressed them, tales of wo that might harrow up a soul with sympathy.

As we sat that evening around the cheerful blaze of the parlor fire, our conversation turned upon the same topics that we had discoursed of in the morning. Mr. Marchion expressed his wonder at the strange and almost miraculous manner in which some persons, who appeared in the very deepest depth of the mire, would become reformed. A little trivial incident—an ordinary occurrence which seemed not worth the importance of a thought—would sometimes change the whole current of their wicked conduct, and present them to the world, regenerated, and disenthralled. One instance, he said, had come to his knowledge in former times, which, if I felt disposed to hear it, he would relate.

I expressed my pleasure at the suggestion, and he commenced his narrative:

"Lift up!" was ejaculated as a signal—and click! went the glasses in the hands of a party of tipsy men, drinking one night at the bar of one of the middling order of taverns. And many a wild gibe was uttered, and many a terrible blasphemy, and many an impure phrase sounded out the pollution of the hearts of those half-crazed creatures, as they tossed down their liquor, and made the walls echo with their uproar. The first and foremost in recklessness was a girlish-faced, fair-haired fellow of twenty-two or three years. They called him Mike. He seemed to be looked upon by the others as a sort of prompter, from whom they were to take cue. And if the brazen wickedness evinced by him in a hundred freaks and remarks to his companions, during their stay in that place, were any test of his capacity—there might hardly be one more fit to go forward as a guide on the road to destruction.

From the conversation of the party, it appeared that they had been spending the earlier part of the evening in a gambling house. The incidents spoken of as having occurred, and the conduct of young Mike and his associates there, are not sufficiently tempting to be narrated.

A second, third and fourth time were the glasses filled, and the effect thereof began to be perceived in a still higher degree of noise and loquacity among the revellers. One of the serving-men came in at this moment, and whispered the bar-keeper, who went out, and in a moment returned again.

"A person," he said, "wished to speak with Mr. Michael. He waited on the walk in front."

The individual whose name was mentioned, made his excuses to the others, telling them he would be back in a moment, and left the room. He had hardly shut the door behind him, and stepped into the open air, when he saw one of his brothers—his elder by eight or ten years—pacing to and fro with rapid and uneven steps. As the man turned in his walk, and the glare of the street lamp fell upon his face; the youth, half-benumbed as his senses were, was somewhat startled at its paleness and evident perturbation.

"Come with me!" said the elder brother, hurriedly, "the illness of our little Jane is worse, and I have been sent for you."

"Poh!" answered the young drunkard, very composedly, "is that all? I shall be home by-and-by."

And he turned to go back again.

"But brother, she is worse than ever before. Perhaps when you arrive she may be *dead*."

The tipsy one paused in his retreat, perhaps alarmed at the utterance of that dread word, which seldom fails to shoot a chill to the hearts of mortals. But he soon calmed himself, and waving his hand to the other:

"Why, see," said he, "a score of times at least, have I been called away to the last sickness of our good little sister; and each time, it proves to be nothing worse than some whim of the nurse or the physician. Three years has the girl been able to live very heartily under her disease; and I'll be bound she'll stay on earth three years longer."

And as he concluded this wicked and most brutal reply, the speaker opened the door and went into the bar-room. But in his intoxication, during the hour that followed, Mike was far from being at ease. At the end of that hour, the words "perhaps when you arrive she may be *dead,*" were not effaced from his hearing yet, and he started for home. The elder brother had wended his way back in sorrow.

Let me go before the younger one, awhile, to a room in that home. A little girl lay there dying. She was quite rational. She had been ill a long time; so it was no sudden thing for her parents, and her brethren and sisters, to be called for the solemn witness of the death agony.

The girl was not what might be called beautiful. And yet, there is a solemn kind of loveliness that always surrounds a sick child. The sympathy for the weak and helpless sufferer, perhaps, increases it in our ideas. The ashiness, and the moisture on the brow, and the film over the eye-balls—what man can look upon the sight and not feel his heart awed within him? Children, I have sometimes fancied too, increase in beauty as their illness deepens. The angels, it may be, are already vesting them with the garments they shall wear in the Pleasant Land.

Beside the nearest relatives of little Jane, standing round her bedside, was the family doctor. He had just laid her wrist down upon the coverlid, and the look he gave the mother, was a look in which there was no hope.

"My child!" she cried, in uncontrollable agony, "my child! you die!"

And the father, and the sons and daughters, were bowed down in grief, and thick tears rippled between the fingers held before their eyes.

Then there was silence awhile. During the hour just bygone, Jane had, in her childish way, bestowed a little gift upon each of her kindred, as a remembrancer when she should be dead and buried in the grave. And there was one of these simple tokens which had not reached its destination. She held it in her hand now. It was a very small, much-thumbed book—a religious story for infants, given her by her mother when she had first learned to read.

While they were all keeping this solemn stillness—broken only by the suppressed sobs of those who stood and watched for the passing away of the girl's soul—a confusion of some one entering rudely and speaking in a turbulent voice, was heard in the adjoining apartment. Again the voice roughly sounded out; it was the voice of the drunkard Mike, and the father bade one of his sons go and quiet the intruder.

"If nought else will do," said he sternly, "put him forth by strength. We want no tipsy brawlers here, to disturb such a scene as this!"

For what moved the sick girl thus uneasily on her pillow, and raised her neck, and motioned to her mother? She would that Mike should be brought to her side. And it was enjoined on him whom the father had bade to eject the noisy one, that he should tell Mike his sister's request, and beg him to come to her.

He came. The inebriate—his mind sobered by the deep solemnity of the scene—stood there, and leaned over to catch the last accents of one who, in ten minutes more, was to be with the spirits of heaven.

All was the silence of deepest night. The dying child held the young man's hand in one of hers; with the other, she slowly lifted the trifling memorial she had assigned especially for him, aloft in the air. Her arm shook—her eyes, now becoming glassy with the death-damps, were cast toward her brother's face. She smiled pleasantly, and as an indistinct gurgle came from her throat, the uplifted hand fell suddenly into the open palm of her brother's, depositing the tiny volume there. Little Jane was dead.

From that night, the young man stepped no more in his wild courses, but was reformed.

When Mr. Marchion concluded his narrative, we sat some minutes in silence. I thought I noticed even more than usual interest concerning it, as he had drawn to its crisis—and I more than half suspected he was himself the young man whose reform had been brought about by the child's death. I was right. He acknowledged, in answer to my questioning, that he had indeed been relating a story, the hero of which was himself.

# XV

*The planter's house was an airy, rustic dwelling, that brought Defoe's description of such places strongly to my recollection. The day was very warm, but the blinds being all closed, a shadowy coolness rustled through the room, which was exquisitely refreshing after the glare and heat without. Before the windows was an open piazza, where, in what they call hot weather—whatever that may be—they sling hammocks, and drink and doze luxuriously.*

DICKENS'S "AMERICAN NOTES"

THE benevolence and good will of the Marchion family, as I have before intimated, led them to pause at nothing which might be of substantial benefit to me. It is almost needless to say that one of the first movements for my improvement, through their means, was my signing the Temperance Pledge. This was, what is in these days called the Old Pledge, which forbade only the drinking of the most ardent kind of liquors, and allowed people to get as much fuddled as they chose upon wines, and beer, and so on. At that time, those who went further, were supposed by many to be altogether too ultra in their views. It will be seen in the remaining chapters of my narrative, whether the Old Pledge was sufficient to remove the dangers which may be apprehended from habits of intemperance. For, though I had now reformed from my hitherto evil courses, and had always subsequently kept the integrity of my promise; I think it will be allowed that the fruits of temperance were not fully reaped by me in that portion of my life, which I am now going to transcribe.

The Marchions supplied me with a moderate portion of funds, and aided me with advice and recommendations in every way. Under their assistance I started myself in a respectable, lucrative, and easy business. I prospered, and the world began to look bright once more.

Some months passed away, when I took a jaunt—partly of business and partly of pleasure—to one of the southern counties of Virginia. In effecting the arrangements I had under my charge, I was now and then forced to wait the convenience of those over whom I had no control. Accordingly, on several occasions, I was detained for days at a time, with no employment on hand except to look about and amuse myself in the best way possible. One of these waiting spells, I well recollect, was at a pleasant, old-settled village, on the banks of a fine stream. I amused the monotony of the time by getting acquainted, as far as I could, with the planters in the neighborhood, and by roaming over their settlements; and even by chatting with the slaves, from whose liveliness and cheerful good-humor, I derived no small share of mirth myself. The Virginians are proverbially hospitable, and friendly to strangers; and taking all things into consideration, the time passed quite as comfortably as I could expect.

One day, I strolled off to some distance beyond the more closely settled part of the village; sauntering lazily along, and having no more particular object in view, than a listless enjoyment of the natural scenery. My walk skirted the banks of the river. Some two miles I had gone on in this way, when I came out upon a little knoll, sloping down to the shore. Upon the highest elevation of the ground, there stood a house, which I could not help admiring for its look of comfort, and the evident good taste which had been active in adorning the grounds and walks around it.

As I walked nearer, to admire some rare plants that stood in pots, by the porch, a middle-aged gentleman came out of the entrance, and saluting me courteously, entered into conversation, and invited me to take a seat in the cool shade of the verandah. My long walk had made me somewhat weary, and I complied with his invitation. I rather thought, from his accent and manner, that he was not an American. In the course of our talk, I learned that he was a bachelor, and had inherited the estate on which he now resided from his father; and that, though somewhat lonely, he generally found sufficient amusement in taking care of the affairs of his plantation. He brought out some excellent wine, before we parted, and we finished a couple of bottles together. It was almost evening when I went away; and then my host, whose name was Bourne, only allowed me to depart under a strict promise, that I would visit him again on the morrow.

Upon my return to the village, I spoke of my entertainment by the planter at whose house I had passed the day, and inquired into his history. I found, from what I learned in the village and in my after acquaintance with the planter himself, that Bourne's father had come over from France, during the troublesome times there, in the latter part of the last century. He was among a large number of gentlemen and citizens, who left that country to obtain quiet, even at the expense of exile. The cause of his departure from his native land, however, was not a disapproval of the schemes of the revolutionizers, just then on the point of coming into power. On the contrary, he assimilated strongly to their doctrines, and afterward took every occasion to instill them into the mind of his son.

Bourne chose America as the place of his retreat, because of the liberty he might enjoy there. And here, where I found my friend of the day before, he had bought himself a plantation, and placed upon it the needful requisites of slaves and material, for the purposes to which he intended applying it.

Perhaps it may hardly be the appropriate place here, to remark upon the national customs of this country; but I cannot help pausing a moment to say that Bourne, as he saw with his own eyes, and judged with his own judgment, became convinced of the fallacy of many of those assertions which are brought against slavery in the south. He beheld, it is true, a large number of men and women in bondage; but he could not shut his eyes to the fact, that they would be far more unhappy, if possessed of freedom. He saw them well taken care of—with shelter and food, and every necessary means of comfort: and he wondered in his own mind, as he remembered what misery he had seen in his travels through various countries of Europe, that the philanthropists of the Old World should wish to interfere with the systems of the New—when the merely nominal oppression of the latter is overbalanced, so many hundred times, by the stern reality of starvation and despotism in the former.

The next day, and for many days after, I was constant in my visits to my new acquaintance. I found him an intelligent and very affable companion; and, as I had yet to stay some weeks in the place, it may easily be supposed I was not at all displeased that such means of amusement were at my command. And the planter, too, seemed highly delighted with our companionship. He had been, as it were, buried from the world, and saw few visiters, except what chance threw in his way.

So intimate did we at length become, and so necessary to one another's comfort, that I took up my residence in his house; and forwarded to New York information, that I should probably not be home during the season. My business there was under the charge of a faithful and competent person, and I had no fear but what all would go right. The letters I had from him, from time to time, presented the most favorable accounts.

Bourne and I, during the day, were much of the time together, and night always found us over a bottle of wine. I fear that, notwithstanding my strict adherence to the pledge I had given, under the advice of the Marchions, the occasions were not a few wherein I was forced to have assistance, in order to reach my chamber.

My residence and walks about the plantation, made me familiar with all its affairs; and I even took upon myself, at times, the direction of things, as though I were upon my own property. I cannot look back upon this period of my life without some satisfaction; though, take it altogether, it was sadly to my detriment that I ever went to Virginia, as will be seen in the sequel. My evil genius was in the ascendant, and worked me harm in a method as singular, as it has ever since been disagreeable to my reflections.

# XVI

*They say 'tis pleasant on the lip,*
*And merry on the brain—*
*They say it stirs the sluggish blood*
*And dulls the tooth of pain.*
*Ay—but within its glowing deeps,*
*A stinging serpent, unseen, sleeps.*

*Its rosy lights will turn to fire,*
*Its coolness change to thirst;*
*And by its mirth, within the brain*
*A sleepless worm is nursed,*
*There's not a bubble at the brim*
*That does not carry food for him.*

WILLIS

AMONG the slaves on Bourne's estate lived a young woman, named Margaret, a creole. She had once been owned by a lady, at whose decease she had been purchased, with others, by the planter, for his farm. The lady had made something of a favorite of the girl, and given her a good education for one of her class. She was of that luscious and fascinating appearance often seen in the south, where a slight tinge of the deep color, large, soft voluptuous eyes, and beautifully cut lips, set off a form of faultless proportions—and all is combined with a complexion just sufficiently removed from clear white, to make the spectator doubtful whether he is gazing on a brunette, or one who has indeed some hue of African blood in her veins. Margaret belonged to the latter class; and she only wanted an opportunity to show, that the fire of her race burnt with all its brightness in her bosom, though smothered by the necessity of circumstances.

The overseer of the business of the plantation, was a man named Phillips. I never liked him—though, as he always treated me well, I could have no occasion to be rude toward him. He was from the north, too—my own section of the country—and with much prudence and industry, he had some of the smaller vices of the human character. His dwelling was a mile, or thereabouts, from Bourne's own residence.

Phillips, it seems, had frequently noticed the beauty of the young slave Margaret, and with a licentious eye. The advances which his situation gave him the means of making, however, had been repulsed, and not always without some appearance of scorn.

It happened, about a week after I took up my abode at the planter's, that Margaret being employed in the field, Phillips came, and, as formerly, offered proposals which the indignant creature rejected with terms of anger. Irritated at her severity, the overseer proceeded to such lengths, that the passionate slave lifted the instrument of labor she had been using, and felled him to the earth with a heavy blow. He lay there senseless, and blood flowed from his wound.

A moment's reflection convinced Margaret of the dangerous nature of the act she had committed. With promptitude, she immediately made up her mind what course to pursue. She came at once to the homestead, and asked for her master. We were sitting together at the time upon the verandah, our usual afternoon retreat. Margaret was ushered there, and told her story. As she went on, I could not help being struck with her beauty, and the influence of the liquor from the bottle by my side, by no means contributed to lessen my admiration.

"If it were to do over again," said the angry girl, her black eye lighted and her cheek mantling with the rich blood, "I would act the same. He knows well enough what I have said before, when he has spoken his wicked words to me, and the consequence of his deeds he can only lay to himself."

My countenance, perhaps, expressed the feelings of admiration I have spoken of; for she looked at me, as if appealing to my influence with Bourne in her behalf. The glance I gave her, in return, conveyed that whatever might be the result of her hasty conduct, she would at least have one defender and advocate—perhaps one whose word would be effectual.

In the course of an hour, Phillips made his appearance at the house, with his head bandaged, and his face quite pallid. He had lost some blood, and that, joined with the hate which now appeared in his face toward the offending slave, gave him an appearance anything but inviting. I did not wonder, as I looked at the man, that Margaret had been so obstinate in her conduct toward him.

The room being turned into a kind of judgment-hall, and each party's side having had its say, Mr. Bourne was perplexed in no small degree as to the decision he should give. Margaret had evidently had more of his good will, as she had of the justice of the dispute; but the planter feared the danger of making a precedent by letting her off triumphantly. He could not bring his conscience to chastise her, and yet something was necessary in the way of punishment. So, leaning partly to justice and partly to expediency, he put on a severe face, lectured the girl upon the enormity of her offence, added a few words and threats—which the grumbling overseer thought smacked far too much of being done merely for effect—and then signified his desire to hear no more upon the subject, by dismissing each one to his or her avocations.

In a day or two the occurrence seemed forgotten. *Seemed* forgotten—but in fact, the pride of Phillips had been wounded too deeply for forgiveness. His breast rankled with feelings of hate toward her who had defied him, and made him a theme of ridicule. There was one other, too, in whose mind the beautiful creole had roused strong thoughts, though of a nature very different from those which dwelt in the soul of the overseer.

I don't know whether I have intimated, in the preceding course of my narrative, that my nature was not wanting in susceptibility to female charms. The truth was so, however. And moreover, I had imbibed not a few of the pernicious notions which prevail among young men in our great American city, upon conjugal matters. My safety, hitherto, had been from the swiftness with which my passion passed over. Often had I been struck with a pretty face—remembered it for four or five days—and then recovered from my delusion to smile at my own folly.

The loveliness and grace of Margaret had fascinated me; but she was one, not of my own race, and her very liberty was owned by another. What had I to do with such as she? Every feeling of prudence and self-respect, spoke loudly in opposition to my allowing any sentiment akin to love for the girl in my bosom, or to express it by my conduct. And yet, strangely enough, I thought nothing of all this; but in my wine-drinking interviews with Bourne, frequently alluded to the subject, and spoke of the regard I had for *his slave.*

There seems to be a kind of strange infatuation, permanently settled over the faculties of those who indulge much in strong drink. It is as frequently seen in persons who use wine, as in them that take stronger draughts. The mind becomes, to use an expressive word, *obfusticated* [obfuscated], and loses the power of judging quickly and with correctness. It seems, too, that the unhappy victim of intemperance cannot tell when he commits even the most egregious violations of right, so muddied are his perceptions, and so darkened are all his powers of penetration. And the worst of it is, that even in his sober moments, the same dark influence hangs around him to a great degree, and leads him into a thousand follies and miseries.

Something of this kind, I presume, was the cause of my conduct, as I am going to relate it. Certainly, a man with his senses about him would never have acted in so absurd a manner. But, *does* an habitual wine-bibber have his senses about him? Not one day out of the weekly seven, but saw Bourne and myself for long hours at the bottle!

In one of these revels, I told my host that my affection for the creole had induced me to come to the determination of marrying her. Instead of placing so singular a proposal in its true colors before me, Bourne expressed his opinion, that if I liked the girl, it would be perfectly proper; and he declared, as an evidence of his friendship for me, that he would give her her freedom that very day. Moreover, a young lad, a brother of Margaret, named Louis, whom the planter also owned, was to be given over to me, as I would probably not like to have it said that a *connection* of mine was a bondsman. For some time we discussed the matter, and arranged it highly to our satisfaction. In truth, before we rose from the table, we were neither of us in a state to know whether we were acting the part of fools or wise men.

Will it be believed? That very afternoon, Bourne, who was a justice of the peace, united myself and the creole in matrimony. The certificate of manumission also was drawn out and signed, and given into Margaret's own hand. A couple of apartments in the homestead were assigned to her use—and I signalized this crowning act of all my drunken vagaries, that night, by quaffing bottle after bottle with the planter.

# XVII

*Haply, for I am black;*
*And have not those soft parts of conversation*
*That chamberers have.*

SHAKESPERE

It needs not that I should particularize the transactions of the next few days. As may reasonably be expected, not a long time elapsed before I awoke from my lethargy. And *when* I awoke! What disgust with myself filled my mind at view of the conduct I had been pursuing! Though since my first chance interview with Bourne, but four or five short weeks had passed away; it seemed, as I looked back over the time, more like an age.

Then I reviewed the uninviting circumstances of my marriage, and my distaste arose toward the creole, *my wife,* who, I felt sure, had done her best to entrap me into all this. The more I thought upon the subject, the more did my dislike to Margaret gain strength. She whom but a little while before, I had looked on with the deepest admiration, was now almost an object of hate to me.

Whatever aversion I felt toward the woman, however, I could not but be conscious of her evident affection to me, as it was exhibited from day to day. She saw and was pained with my conduct. She tried a thousand fond arts to gain back the love I had once shown for her. She conducted herself in the most decorous and humble manner. But all to no avail.

Was my former love for the creole, then, become totally extinct? Ah, human love, to be lasting, must be pure and worthily bestowed.

The course of my narrative needs now that another character should be introduced upon the stage. My evil destiny would have it, that an old city acquaintance of mine, Mrs. Conway, a widow lady, visited the neighborhood at this time, and took up her quarters in the house of the overseer Phillips, to whom she was distantly related. I had met the lady often at the house of persons whom I knew in New-York; and of course nothing was more natural than for me to call upon her.

Mrs. Conway was about twenty-five, and very handsome; not with unformed and unripened loveliness, but in the rich swell, the very maturity of personal perfection. Her light hair, blue eyes, and the delicacy of her skin, formed a picture rarely met with in that region; and perhaps on this very account, the more prized. She was a woman of the world, however. Gifted with such singular charms, and her mind ornamented with the most needful and complete culture; she had but one aim, the conquest of hearts. And seldom did she determine to make any individual addition to her adorers, but what her efforts were crowned with triumph. Luckless were the stars that led her southward!

The very next day after this woman came among us, she made up her mind to bring *me* to her feet. Probably it was partly from natural inclination, and partly to find herself some agreeable method of dissipating monotony, that caused the lady to form this determination. She (I afterward found out all this) mentioned the project to her relative, Phillips, who approved of it, and promised to give it any aid in his power. He had never forgotten the indignity bestowed on him by Margaret, before she became raised to her present situation. Policy afterward led him to disguise his feelings; but they were by no means effaced.

It needs not to explain all the artifices which were used for effecting what the plotters desired to accomplish. Fortunately for them, they had a willing subject to work upon; and in much less time than they could have anticipated, I was indeed in the toils.

I do not think I admired Mrs. Conway; at least, I did not at first. But I felt no small disposition to feign that sentiment, if it were merely to mortify my ill-assorted wife. For my dissatisfaction at the marriage was of much longer continuance than my love for the creole; and though I felt ashamed to show the people of the household how bitterly I repented of my drunken rashness—for the marriage deserved no other name—I felt sick at heart whenever I thought upon it. We lived together, Margaret and I, but there was often little of peace and pleasure between us.

"I fear that northern beauty has bewitched you," said Margaret, with a smile, as I returned one evening from calling at the overseer's; "you did not use to be so partial to Mr. Phillips's pathway."

"Matters of business," answered I, a little confused; "nothing but business."

"But is she really as handsome as I hear? I have been told by our people, that fancy can hardly conceive any creature more perfect."

"You have been told the truth," said I; "she is wonderfully fair, not dark and swarthy, which I detest!" and I turned away, sure of the effect of the sharp arrow I had winged.

"Indeed!" burst from the surprised Margaret; and she would have spoken further, but her pride came to prevent her.

Surely, a few short days could not have made this sudden change in my affections. And then the creole thought of many little things that had before been airy trifles, but were now too sure a groundwork for her suspicions.

The fears of the jealous woman were to be consummated but too soon, leaving her no further ground to doubt. I shortly made no secret of my attachment to Mrs. Conway. Indeed, I believe that, as it often happens in similar cases, the feeling I began by dissembling, I after awhile really felt in truth. Like an actor who plays a part, I became warmed in the delineation, and the very passion I feigned, came to imbue my soul with its genuine characteristics.

Poor Margaret! it was a wild and fearful storm that raged within her bosom, when she came fully to know the truth of her desertion. I have no doubt she had loved me tenderly, ever since the time of my interference in her behalf when she was arraigned for striking Phillips; and with all the fiery disposition of her nation, she now felt torn with strong passions, to think that another had supplanted her. I do not think I have given a faithful transcript of the creole's character in all its strong points. She was, indeed, a very woman, with some of the most beautiful traits, and some of the most devilish that ever marked her sex. Her ambition of rising above the low level of her companions, had been gratified by the act wherein Bourne conferred freedom upon her. Such freedom had been one of the dearest dreams of her life. And to be the wife of one who occupied a respectable station among the masters of the land, was an exalted destiny beyond which her hopes could hardly rise,

She felt that her being a free woman, gave her much power by the law; and that I was bound to her by indissoluble ties. But with excellent policy, she never allowed her knowledge of this to appear in her conversation or conduct. She had a most difficult part to play; and, as I have in late years, cast my mind back, I could not help being struck with wonder at the dexterous manner in which she avoided many a quicksand, and kept from an open rupture with me, where we had so little in common. Hapless girl! I would that her destiny might have been a more fortunate one!

# XVIII

*No man is safe, who drinks. Actions which are the height of injustice, are often committed under the influence of liquor, to those whom we are bound to cherish.*

TEMPERANCE ADDRESS

WHETHER Mrs. Conway returned my admiration, and whether she would have accepted the offer of my hand, had I been in a fit condition to give it, I cannot say. The probability is, however, that in our intercourse the same current of events took place which I have described in my own case. In the first stages, she no doubt acted the part of a most unqualified coquet. But in our subsequent meetings, she may have been touched by the ardency of my love, which was more intense, as it might have been called more legitimate, than that I had borne the creole.

As I gazed on the widow's bewitching beauty—her soft sunny complexion, and her mild eyes—as I listened to her conversation, charming for itself alone, and doubly so from the musical tones it flowed in—I felt myself steeped indeed in the extacy of passion.

One day, after drinking with Bourne, I had been visiting the widow, and pouring into her ears some of those wild thoughts and protestations which wine and love can generate. The beauty listened complacently, for when was homage distasteful to a woman? All of a sudden, a capricious thought entered her brain.

"Come!" said she to me, "I wonder if you would prove, by something more tangible than words, the reality of all this fine sentiment?"

"If there is anything, lady, you wish done," I replied, "that mortal man can do, I will attempt it."

And I spoke with an energy that showed my mind.

"In a stroll I took two or three days since," continued the widow, "I saw a fine boy of some eight or nine years old. They told me he belonged to you. Now I fancy I should like just such a little fellow to be my page, after the fashion of the damsels of old."

"What was his name?" asked I.

"They called him Louis. And now I think of it, some one said he was the brother of the woman Margaret, who lives at your dwelling."

I started, and felt the blood rushing up in my face like fire. Could the widow have intended to strike that chord? Louis was indeed the brother of the creole, and was beloved by her, as a woman might cling to her own child.

The widow waited for an answer several moments in vain.

"How soon gallantry cools when its labor or its money is required!" she said at length, with a contemptuous smile.

"Forgive me, lady, it is not that," and I spoke very earnestly, "it is not that. Ask of me something else. There are reasons," added I, in a quick and confused voice, "reasons I may not mention why that request must be denied. But some other surely will do as well. There are many children among the slaves, and you shall have your choice of them all."

The widow knew the reasons I alluded to full well.

"My choice is made," she replied, calmly and coolly; "it was but an idle notion, and I have done wrong to trouble you with it."

"I beg you," rejoined I, "let some other take the boy's place in your wish."

"Speak no more about it, sir"; the lady answered, in a tone as if intended to cut short the subject; "it is not worth your while to think of a silly woman's whims. Though I don't know, indeed, which are worse—false words, or foolish fancies. I beg you, speak no more about it."

But I did speak further about it. I entreated her to select some other, any dozen others, instead of Louis. Her answer was still the same.

Those who have read the preceding chapters of this narrative, and who know the great failing which has attended me from my very outset of life—weakness of resolution, and liability to be led by others—can conceive the result of this interview. Before I left the widow, I promised to comply with her request about the boy. He was mine, I argued, and why should I not do with my own property as I liked, and bestow it as I listed?

The creole, I have said, loved her young brother very fondly. Who may describe, then, what took place in her bosom when this matter was broken to her? At first it caused a kind of stunning sensation of surprise, almost of incredulity. Then came the tempest. All the fearful propensities which had slumbered so long in her soul, were aroused. Was this stranger—this fair-faced interloper from abroad, not only to destroy the love which had been to her as life; but her very brother to be taken away and made a servant, for *her* beck and command? What right had she, this delicate child of another climate, to invade the privileges and the happiness that had been so pleasant? The spirit of her fiery race swelled in the creole's breast, as she thought of these things: and she cursed her rival with a sharp and bitter tongue.

Louis was sent to his new mistress. Before the time of his departure, his sister was observed to have several long and close interviews with him. What the subject of those interviews was, they alone knew.

At length came the capstone of the misfortunes of Margaret. Rumors floated to her ear of preparations for an intended divorce between myself and her, and of a marriage in prospect of the widow and me. The latter part of the story was an addition of the busy tongue of common report.

The creole occupied the same apartments in the homestead yet: but their accommodations were no longer shared by me. I spent a great portion of my time at the overseer's. Bourne was busy with his plantation, it being a season when its weal depended on his active supervision. We had our daily drinking-bouts, however, and our friendship was as firmly knit as it had ever been.

As I sometimes glance back at this period of my life, I think with more regret and dissatisfaction upon it, than upon any other portion of my conduct. My early follies were the result of inexperience in the ways of the world, and of the errors of impulse; hardly any of them but have some excuse. They were either committed or begun when I was under the influence of liquor, and had lost the control of my faculties; or were forced upon me by circumstances, and might be attributed to the great failing I have before alluded to—weakness of resolution. But my acts during the few weeks I resided at Bourne's, were done more in the method of deliberate and premeditated folly. I had my eyes open, and still went on, as though I were blindfolded.

The true explanation of the mystery is, I think, to be found in my former, and present habits of drinking spirituous liquors. Those habits were of the most insidious, sly, and fatal detriment to me. They relaxed my energy of character, what little I had, and left me like a ship upon the ocean, without her mainmast. I was tossed about by every breeze of chance or impulse, and was guilty of a hundred foolish things, which the relation of makes my story appear indeed like a work of imagination, instead of what it honestly is, a record of real events. So evil are the consequences of dissipation!

I can trace the outset of all these frailties, as well as all the calamities that have befallen me in my life, to that fatal night when Colby drew me into the drinking place; where, amid music and gayety, the first step in my downward road was taken.

# XIX

*In vain the flattering verse may breathe*
*Of ease from pain, and rest from strife;*
*There is a sacred dread of death,*
*Inwoven with the strings of life.*

BRYANT

WHILE matters were in the situation described in the last few paragraphs, a danger was preparing, that threatened destruction not only to the love of myself and the widow, but to our lives, and the lives of the whole family and neighborhood. One of those epidemical diseases that prevail in the South made its appearance, and began to spread in all directions. Alarm and consternation fell upon the people. Beginning at first with striking down a man here and there, the fearful Plague Spirit, after a time, became as it were insatiate in his demands.

At the first appearance of the scourge, Mrs. Conway would have flown back to her native north. I, however, to whom her presence had become very dear, represented the evil as far less than rumor attempted to make it. I smiled at her terrors, and though my own heart accused me of untruth, I told the widow that there was little danger.

Thus she remained in fancied security, until it was too late. When the real facts could no longer be kept from her knowledge, it was quite as dangerous to leave as to remain. And yet, so deeply seated was this woman's love of admiration, that she really forgave me for deceiving her, in consideration of the motive that led me to be guilty of it.

One of the last places where the sickness came, was the village near Bourne's plantation. It was a place of not much travel, and being in a more than ordinarily healthy location, its inhabitants had flattered themselves with a hope of escaping the pestilence which desolated their fellow towns. Vain were their hopes. One day authentic information was brought to the planter, that the disease had made its appearance there; and, unfortunately for him, its first stroke was levelled at a poor family whose house stood near the confines of his estate. He was advised to be very cautious, and furthermore enjoined by his medical attendant, who sent the information just mentioned, that fear and anxiety concerning the matter were precisely the things that would bring about the result most dreaded.

All this was kept from Mrs. Conway's ears. I already began to blame myself for my deceit. I took every earthly means to guard her from the dangers that surrounded the place, and never allowed her to hear aught that might produce in her mind those disturbed thoughts which the physician deprecated. New to the climate, and more liable than a native to its deleterious influences, I knew she would stand little chance of recovery, if once attacked by the dreaded malady.

But amid the general alarm and precaution, there was one person who paid small heed to either. That person was the deserted Margaret. She cared little about bodily danger, for she pined in a deeper rooted sorrow, and not only pined, but with feelings of one much injured, she fostered in her soul the desire of retribution on her injurer. Me, she could not bring herself to regard with any other passion than fondness; but her rival was hated with as deep a loathing, as ever swelled the soul of a jealous woman.

When she heard of the epidemic, her first thought was a desire that the widow would be one of its victims. When the news was brought that it had broken out in our immediate neighborhood, she arranged in her mind a scheme, subtle and worthy the brain whence it sprung—a scheme of revenge. The whole of the thoughts and conduct of the woman, though at the time unknown to me, were afterward fixed too firmly in my knowledge and my memory.

The next day, Louis, her brother, came to the planter's house on some errand for his mistress. Whether that errand required his sister's personal attention or not, I cannot say; but for a long time the child was closetted with Margaret in her apartment. As he left the place, there flashed in his eye a spice of lurking devil, which spoke him to be not a slack partaker of his sister's soul.

Down one of the winding-lanes of Bourne's plantation, that very afternoon, two figures were slowly walking. One was a lady, passing beautiful; the other was a boy, a fine-looking youth, his cheeks tinged with a slight color, betraying though feebly his taint of African blood. The lady was Mrs. Conway; the boy, her attendant Louis.

"It is pleasant," said the widow, "to get once more a taste of the open air; I have been cooped up so long, that it comes to me like something strange and unwonted."

The boy walked on near her in silence.

"Do you not think, Lewy, we are strangely kept in by Mr. Bourne's and Mr. Evans's whims? It was but the other day the latter told me not to stir out of the house to a distance on any account. You don't have robbers here, I hope?"

"I never knew of one about the place, in all my life," answered the child.

"And this sickness," said the lady, "what a fearful thing if it should appear among us! They say, boy, such as I, coming from another clime, stand a double danger from it."

The child looked up in his companion's face with a strange look; and continued to walk on in silence.

"How sweet the air is!" continued the lady. It was more like talking to herself than a listener; but the foible of her sex is proverbial, and Mrs. Conway was no exception to any of her sex's foibles. "How sweet the air is! Life seems pleasant in the South, if it be only for the mild, warm air. Then, the beautiful flowers bloom all around, and are reared with so little trouble; and you have rich fruit here, such as never grows in the rigor of our stormy north. But as much as anything else, I love to hear the birds—the sweet singing birds of the South!"

"What do you think of a bird that can sing tunes?" asked Louis, suddenly.

"I think he would be well worth owning," said the lady.

"Would you like to see such a bird?" rejoined the boy, looking up into Mrs. Conway's face, and with something like a tremor in his voice.

"Certainly," said she, smiling at what appeared to be his childish earnestness; "I would like any variation, however small, of the sameness of this quiet life. Where shall we find the curiosity of which you speak?"

"Through the path yonder," answered Louis, "a little beyond that wood. Andy Warner lives there, and he has the bird hung up in a cage in his room."

"Come on then," said the widow, laughing: "Andy Warner shall show us this prodigy."

And she motioned to go; but the child stirred not. His eyes stared in a wild manner, and he trembled from head to foot.

"How, boy?" exclaimed the lady. "What is the matter? You are sick, Louis, you are sick, I fear!"

"No, I am quite well," answered he, recovering his former appearance. "Come, let us go on to Andy's."

They walked down the lane, and along the path which Louis pointed out. It led to a kind of bye-place. The house he had mentioned was situated at some distance from the principal wagon-way, and on the present occasion, exhibited no sign of tenancy or life. They knocked at the door, which after a moment or two was opened by a woman, who received them with a look so full of startling surprise, that Mrs. Conway knew not what to make of it. They told the woman the reason of their visit—and then she stood looking at them again, in a second long stare of wonder and wildness.

"There!" said Louis, pointing with his finger, "there is the bird!"

Mrs. Conway glanced up, and beheld one of the southern mocking birds, in a cage attached to the wall. The little songster seemed in a sulky vein, however; he hung his head and was totally without cheerfulness or animation.

"Could you make him sing some gay, lively strain now?" said the visiter, turning to her hostess with a sprightly air.

As she looked more fully in the face of the one to whom she spoke, Mrs. Conway started back in alarm. The woman seemed like a ghost—her face pale, and her whole aspect bearing an indescribable appearance of strangeness and insanity. Mrs. Conway was instantly impressed with the idea that she was deranged, and turned in alarm to leave the room.

"Good God!" exclaimed the pale-faced female, "she talks here of singing gay strains!"

Fairly terrified, the widow now made a quick exit, and only recovered her self-possession when she found herself in the open air with Louis by her side. They walked swiftly along the path on their return; for the day was now somewhat advanced, and they had strayed quite a distance from Phillips's house.

That very afternoon I had called at the overseer's, and been told that Mrs. Conway was out on a walk. I started forth to look for her, that I might accompany her back. So it happened, that as she came by the dwelling of Bourne, near which she had to pass, I met her.

She immediately began telling me of her afternoon's adventure. As she mentioned the course of her walk, I started, for a dim fear took possession of my mind, to which I dared not give credit, and yet thought too probable.

"But never mind," exclaimed the widow, in continuation, as she finished her story, "I suppose Andy Warner will be at home himself some day, and then I shall, no doubt, get treated with more politeness."

"Did you," gasped I faintly, as the name struck my ear, and a feeling of deadly sickness crept over my heart—"did you say Andy——?"

I staggered and clutched the air, as a man grasping support to keep from falling.

"Did you say Andy Warner?" came up again from my throat in a hoarse whisper.

"Yes, yes, that was the name, I think"; and the alarmed lady turned with an inquiring look to Louis.

"Then you are lost, indeed," cried I, in tones of shrieking horror. "In that house was the first case of the horrid fever. Andy *died* this very morning, and if you had looked farther, you would no doubt have found his corpse, for it lies there yet!"

One moment more, and a wild shrill cry sounded out upon the air, waking the echoes, and sailing off in many a sharp cadence. Another followed—and another—and the widow sank down upon the grass in a senselessness so deep, that I thought the contagion would have no chance of working its effect upon her. I was almost out of my senses with agony and alarm. But time pressed, and lifting that form so dear to me, in my arms, I bore her into the planter's residence, and there had those attentions paid which the urgency of the case demanded. In an hour, the widow was somewhat recovered from her fit. But she was still as languid as a babe, and the physician who had been summoned, spoke strongly against the propriety of carrying her the mile's distance which intervened between the house, and Phillips's residence.

So I had it arranged that she should not be removed. In the south range of apartments, there was one with long low windows, opening to the ground. That room was prepared for her reception and there I had her carried.

# XX

*Thou sure and firm-set earth,*
*Hear not my steps which way they walk for fear;*
*The very stones prate of my whereabout,*
*And take the present horror from the time,*
*Which now suits with it.*

SHAKSPERE

COULD it be possible that the widow might escape the fatal effects of her visit to the cottage? Whatever chance there might have been for some other more equable mind, I saw that her agitation and ceaseless fear left none for her.

Before the end of the second day after that hapless walk, the signs of the coming horrors appeared on her cheek. They were the signals for a general desertion on the part of the attendants. So great was the panic struck to the souls of people by the stories they had heard of the pestilence, that I found it difficult to get for Mrs. Conway the attentions absolutely necessary to her existence. Even before the disease had made its complete appearance, the servants refused to go near her. The unhappy woman had, however, one most devoted servant. Night and day was I ready at the entrance of her apartment, holding a sleepless watch over its inmate.

I shall not think it worth while for my story to give a minute account of the lady's illness. The sick chamber is a scene which few love to look upon, or to have pictured for them. The sight of this beautiful tabernacle with its foundations broken, and its mysterious furniture out of place, and its strength bowed down in weakness—whose eye has such unhealthy craving as to delight in the grievous spectacle? The soul of a man loves its dwelling, and though itself not thereof, looks on when that dwelling is harmed by evil, and feels in its recesses a sympathizing sorrow.

At length the time arrived, which at some period or other arrives for all cases of bodily disease—the time of the crisis. The doctor came, and with a wise look, told the listeners that his patient was at the most dangerous part of her malady. He prepared some mixtures of his nauseous drugs, gave directions about the order of their being administered, and then closed by remarking to me that, in the course of the evening or night, the suffering lady would probably fall into a continued slumber, from which she would awake to a new life, or to death.

And where was Margaret of late? The wretched creole lived in her former situation, as far as locality was concerned; but her heart and her happiness were fled for ever. She seldom left her rooms, staying there almost alone, and brooding over her griefs and her injuries, which fancy made many times greater than they really were.

It seems to have been the case, that with this creature's good traits her heart had still a remnant of the savage. When Mrs. Conway's illness appeared favorable, Margaret's bosom felt heavy and sorrowful; and when the sick woman was hovering on the confines of the grave, the other's soul danced with a joyous feeling of life.

When the creole heard that the doctor announced the critical period to have arrived—and heard also what was said about the probable lethargy—the discarded favorite asked her informant again. Receiving the same account, she sat a full minute, apparently gazing on some vision in the air. At length, it seemed to melt from her sight; she drew a heavy breath, and resumed her ordinary appearance.

The God of Mysteries only can tell what passions worked in the woman's breast then, and during the rest of that fearful night. What deep breathings of hate—what devilish self-incitements,—what unrelenting, yet swaying resolves—what sanguinary brain-thoughts—what mad, and still clearly defined marking out of fiendish purposes—what of all these raged and whirled in the chambers of that unhappy creature's soul, will ever stay buried in the darkness of things gone: a darkness which falls alike on the dreadful motives of the murderer, and the purity of hearts filled with abundance of good!

Midnight hung its curtains round about the planter's dwelling. Sleep and Repose were there with their pleasant ministerings, and Silence, the handmaiden of both. In the chamber of the sick one there was a lamp, sending forth its feeble beams, and looking as if it were about to gasp its last gasp—ominous emblem of the life that lay flickering near. From the bed which held the beautiful sufferer, sounded breathings faint but regular. There was no nurse or watcher there, for the physician had said it was of no importance, and all were worn out with their long-continued attending upon the invalid. Even I myself had sunk into a deep sleep at the door of the room, exhausted nature refusing to allow any further demand upon her powers.

One of the long windows was partly open, and only a thin piece of gauze was between the ground to which it led and the room. At that window appeared, time and again, two bright small orbs, fixed, and yet rolling in fire. Ever and anon they would draw back into the shadow; then again they would peer inward upon the room, their direction ever being to the bed whereon the sick one lay.

It was wrong to say that couch had no watcher! Three long hours did those glittering things, which were human eyes, continue to keep the vigils of that noiseless spot. Three long hours, while hardly a motion, except the swaying back and forth, before spoken of, disturbed the constancy of their gaze, or a sound broke the solemn stillness.

In the deep hour of that night the widow awoke; and as she awoke, her cool blood, for the first time during five days, coursed through veins that did not throb with loathsome heat. Then she knew that she should live.

All around was motionless and soundless, and the lady felt glad that it was so; for her heart was in that mood of blissful calm to which the least jar produces pain.

"Thank God!" sounded in a low murmur from her tongue; "thank God! I shall not die!"

The sounds came faintly; but faint as they were, they sank into ears besides those of the speaker. They sank and pierced, with a dagger's sharpness, the soul of Margaret, the creole; for she it was, whose eyes had been during those long three hours almost winkless at the room window.

And was her rival, then, to get well once more? And were all her late hopes to vanish? That pale-browed northerner *married* to him she loved? Never should the sun rise upon that marriage!

Horrid purposes lighted up the creole's eyes as she softly put aside the curtains, and stepped into the room. With a stealthy pace she drew near to the sick woman's bed. One moment she paused. The widow lay there, still very beautiful, and calm as a sleeping infant. As Margaret approached, the invalid turned and looked at her a moment, but it was plain she knew her not, and probably thought her to be some hired attendant.

Still nearer and nearer came the wretched female: and now she stands by the very bedside. Unconscious yet, the lady is quiet and composed—fearing nothing and suspecting nothing. An instant more, and her throat is clutched by a pair of tight-working hands. Startled with terror, she would shriek, but cannot. What torture fills her heart! She turns, and struggles, and writhes; but those deadly fingers loosen not their grasp.

The murderess presses upon her. Poor lady! Her soul feels very sick, as in one little minute whole troops of remembrances, and thoughts, and dreads, come over her. She grows fainter and fainter. Her struggles become less energetic, and her convulsive writhings cease. Still those terrible hands release not. Their suffocating span is continued yet for several minutes.

And now, no longer is it necessary that Margaret should keep her hold; that last faint gurgle tells the consummation of the fell design. Her deed is done. Her revenge triumphs!

Like some ghost condemned to wander on earth for the actions done there, a figure stalked about the garden and the grounds near by, during the remainder of that night. Bright stars shone down, and the cool breeze swept by; but the Shape heeded them not, walking swiftly on in zigzag directions, apparently without any particular point of destination. Sometimes stretching off down a lane, and stopping by the fence, and leaning thereon, and looking at the cattle that lay doubled on the grass reposing: sometimes bending over a flower, and taking it very carefully and inhaling its fragrance; and sometimes standing like a marble statue, motionless, and gazing vacantly for a long time in the bodiless air: these were the freaks of the strange figure.

It was the murderess who wandered there and thus. And as the first streak of light appeared in the east, she started like the guilty thing she was, and returned to her abiding place.

# XXI

*I'll tell you friend, what . . .*
*Where'er I scan this scene of life*
*Inspires my waking schemes,*
*And, when I sleep, . . .*
*Dances before my ravished sight,*
*In sweet, aërial dreams.*

PROFESSOR FRISBIE

How refreshing it is to pause in the whirl and tempest of life, and cast back our minds over past years! I think there is even a kind of satisfaction in deliberately and calmly reviewing actions that we feel were foolish or evil. It pleases us to know that we have the learning of experience. The very contrast, perhaps, between what we are, and what we were, is gratifying. At all events, it is acknowledged that retrospection becomes one of the delights of people immediately after arriving at mature years. When merely on the verge of manhood, we love to think of the scenes of our boyish life. When advanced in age, we fondly turn our memory to the times of the early years, and dwell with a chastened pleasure upon what we recollect thereof, beheld through the medium of the intervening seasons.

From no other view can I understand how it is, that I sometimes catch myself turning back in my reflection, to the very dreariest and most degraded incidents which I have related in the preceding pages, and thinking upon them without any of the bitterness and mortification which they might be supposed to arouse in my bosom. The formal narration of them, to be sure, is far from agreeable to me—but in my own self-communion upon the subject, I find a species of entertainment. I was always fond of day-dreams—an innocent pleasure, perhaps, if not allowed too much latitude.

For some days after Mrs. Conway's death, I shut myself up in my room, and hardly went out at all, except in the evening, or early morning. A kind of morbid peculiarity came over me during this while, which, though it fortunately passed off with a change of scene, was very powerful for the time. It was the result, no doubt, partly of my confinement and the sombre reflections I held—and partly of my former intemperate habits. It was a species of imaginative mania, which led to giving full scope to my fancy—and I frequently remained for two hours at a time in a kind of trance, beholding strange things, and abstracted from all which was going on around me. On one of these occasions, the incident occurred which I shall now relate.

I was sitting in an easy chair at twilight one evening, near the open window. Upon my knees lay a newspaper, which I had been reading. It contained some extracts from an eloquent temperance address. The quietness of the scene, and the subdued light, and the peculiar influences that had been surrounding me for a few days past, had their full chance to act at such a time, as may well be imagined.

Methought I was wandering through the cities of a mighty and populous empire. There were sea-ports, filled with rich navies, and with the products of every part of the earth, and with merchants, whose wealth was greater than the wealth of princes. There were huge inland towns, whose wide and magnificent avenues seemed lined with palaces of marble—and showed on every side the signs of prosperity. I saw from the tops of the fortresses, the Star-Flag—emblem of Liberty—floating gloriously abroad in the breeze!

And how countless were the inhabitants of that country! On I went, and still on, and they swarmed thicker than before. It was almost without boundary, it seemed to me—with its far-stretching territories, and its States away up in the regions of the frozen north, and reaching down to the hottest sands of the torrid south—and with the two distant oceans for its side limits.

With the strange faculty of dreams, I knew, that two-score years had elapsed, as I stood amid this mighty nation. I was in one of their greatest cities—and there appeared to be some general holyday. People were hurrying up and down the streets. The children were dressed in gay clothes. Business seemed to be suspended—and each one given up to the spirit of the time.

"Is it not," I heard one of the passers by say to a companion, "is it not a glorious thing?"

"Most glorious!" said the second.

I lost all further hearing of their remarks, for they walked on, smiling in each other's faces.

Before long, following a crowd, I came into a wide open kind of amphitheatre, where a man stood up in the midst addressing the assembly. The address seemed to be preparatory to something which was to take place at its conclusion.

"The Snake-Tempter," said the man who was speaking, "is this day to be deprived of his last vassal! Long, long have we looked for the coming of this day. It has been our hope, our beacon of encouragement through seasons of toil and darkness. Who would have supposed, years ago, that it could so soon have arrived?

"Now man is free! He walks upon the earth, worthy the name of one whose prototype is God! We hear the mighty chorus sounding loud and long, Regenerated! Regenerated!

"Oh, could those who have wrought and sickened for the coming of this hour—could they but be present with us—how would their hearts leap with joy! But do we know that they are *not* present with us? Who can tell that their spirits may not be soaring in the viewless air near by, and looking down pleasantly upon us, and blessing us? Who can say, but that they are rejoicing in their hearts, and praising the Almighty that these things have come to pass?

"The last vassal of the Tempter is indeed lost him. This day, our charter receives the name of him who finishes the

Great Work! We can say then, that of all who live among us, there is none but has his title upon the bond, and his claim to its prerogative."

For some time, the man went on in this strain. Then the assembly dispersed, apparently for the purpose of engaging in the other ceremonies of the occasion.

I had wandered to and fro for an hour or more, when I came out in a wide street, to the sides of which I saw the people flocking from every quarter. Away in the distance there sounded bands of music, which grew louder and louder, as if they were coming toward us.

At length a long and splendid procession was seen, marching with stately pace. First came a host of men in the prime of life, with healthy faces and stalwart forms, and every appearance of vigor. They had many banners, which bore mottoes, signifying that they had once been under the dominion of the Tempter, but were now redeemed. Then I saw a myriad of youths, with blooming cheeks and bright eyes, who followed in the track of those before, as in time they no doubt would occupy their stations in the world. There were rich equipages, also, containing the officers of the state, and persons of high rank. Long, long it stretched, and still there seemed no end.

Not the least beautiful part of the procession, was composed of bands of women and young girls, dressed with taste, and lending their smiles to enliven the scene. I saw many children also, whose happy and innocent looks were pleasant to behold.

All through the long sweep of the multitude, there were innumerable banners, and mottoes, and devices, expressive of triumph and rejoicing. One of them, I noticed, had the figure of a fair female, robed in pure white. Under her feet were the senseless remains of a hideous monster, in whose grapple thousands and millions had fallen, but who was now powerless and dead. The eyes of the female beamed benevolence and purity of heart; and in her hand she held a goblet of clear water.

Toward the end of the march came a large car, upon which was a single personage, a man of middle age, who, as he passed along, was saluted by the shouts of the crowd. He seemed to be the theme, in fact, of all the ceremonials and the rejoicing.

"Who is he?" said I to a by-stander. "Who is he, for whom the people raise their voices so loudly?"

The man turned to me in amazement.

"Have you not heard," he answered, "of the great triumph of this day? The one upon the car is the Last Vassal of the Snake-Tempter; and he goes now to make a formal renunciation of his old allegiance."

"And is this the cause, then, of all the public joy?" said I.

"It is," answered the man.

How it was, I cannot say, but I understood his meaning, though he spoke with strange phrases.

So, yielding myself to the passage of those about, I wended on, until at last we came into a wide field, in the middle of which was an uncovered scaffold. Upon it was the person whom I had noticed in the procession—the Last Vassal. Far around, on every side, countless multitudes of nothing but human heads were to be seen, in one compact body.

"Rejoice!" cried a man from the crowd. "Our old enemy is deserted, and we triumph!"

Then there arose such mighty shouts from the huge concourse, that it seemed as if the sound might pierce the very heavens.

And now, he who stood on the scaffold spoke:

"It gladdens me," he said, "that I shall this day make one of the Army of the Regenerated. You have wrought long and faithfully, and your reward comes in good time. It is well."

Loud shouts evinced the pleasure of the multitude at hearing him utter such remarks.

"We welcome you!" they cried, as with one voice.

"This day," continued he, "I throw off the chains, and take upon myself the pleasant bondage of good. It may not be a truth to boast of, that I am the *last* of the serfs of Appetite; yet I joy that I occupy my position before you now, as I do!"

A venerable old man came forward upon the scaffold, and presented a document to the speaker. He received it with evident delight; and snatching a pen from a table, he wrote his name under it, and held it up to the view of the people.

It were impossible to describe the thunder-peal of hurrahs that arose in the air, and sounded to the skies, as the Full Work was consummated thus. They cried aloud—

"Victory! victory! The Last Slave of Appetite is free, and the people are regenerated!"

# XXII

*This even-handed justice*
*Commends the ingredients of our poisoned chalice*
*To our own lips.*

SHAKSPERE

UPON the distraction which filled my breast, when it was found in the morning that the widow had died—and the burial of the body—and the cunning smoothness of the Creole during the intervening time—I shall bestow no more than this passing mention. Whether any suspicions of foul play were as yet aroused in the breasts of other persons, is more than I can say. As far as I was concerned, however, I had not the most distant idea of the kind; and taking all things into reflection, the likelihood is that no one thought Mrs. Conway's death, under the circumstances, aught more than was to have been expected.

But guilt has a vital power, which gives it life, until it is held up to scorn. It happened so in this case. Louis, the brother of Margaret, was taken sick with the same disease of which the widow was supposed to have died. Strangely enough, when the Creole plotted with the boy to entice his mistress into the infected cottage (for that occurrence was the result of design,) she did not think how the danger would be shared by Louis too. Her soul had strained its gaze with the single purpose of revenge; and she saw not each incidental effect. Thus it is with evil intentions. I have noticed that the bad are always short-sighted in the plots they form, and the manoeuvres they engage in, some little thing or other escapes their view, and proves, after a while, to be a seed of punishment and remorse.

Again the curtains of darkness hung around the planter's dwelling; and again had the balancing point of the sickness arrived for a sufferer there. That sufferer was little Louis. He had left the house of the overseer, and now lived at his old abode. There was the same breathlessness and the same want of movement, as on the preceding occasion; but instead of the sick room being almost deserted, as in the former case, many persons waited there. Perhaps they had become more callous to fear, because it was not a new thing; perhaps it was, that they thought the influences of a sick child's apartment more gentle and less dangerous than the former one. Margaret stood in a position so quiet, and with eyes so stony in their gaze, that she seemed like one entranced. On the result of the pending sleep of her brother, it seemed as if her reason and her life were wavering.

At last the slumberer awoke. The Creole shrieked! for it was plain Louis but aroused himself a moment, to sink shortly in that deep senselessness which knows no waking here on earth. He shifted himself uneasily on his bed. A film came over Margaret's eyes—a film of fear and agony; and when it passed off and left her sight clear, she saw, lying before her, the quiet ghastly corpse of her brother.

Those who were present felt awed at her terrible grief. She screamed aloud, and threw her arms around the boy, and pressed his forehead to her lips. She called him by all the old endearing epithets, and seemed crazed with her sense of desperate sorrow. The wild exclamations that started from her mouth, the listeners heard with wonder.

"Do not go!" she said, looking on the inanimate form of the boy. "Do not go. The pleasant days are not all past. If you leave me, my heart will crack!"

Then in a whisper:

"O, never tell me of her kindness. Lead her into the hut, I say. She is a witch, and can steal hearts."

She paused, and looked intently at some phantom before her.

"Why, how long she sleeps! She shall sleep longer, though, and deeper, after to-night. Softly! softly! softly!"

The heart-strings were too much wrought, and the Creole sank heavily down upon the floor, in a fit. Those who stood by looked strangely into each other's faces, but no one spoke.

It was evident that something wrong had been done, and weighed heavily on the wretched woman's mind. Her words, and her strange gestures could not but have a meaning to them. Gossipping tongues, once started upon such matters, are not easily put to rest; and before long the dark rumor came to Mr. Phillips's ear that his kinswoman had been murdered—murdered by her, too, on whom, of all who lived around, he wished an opportunity of showing his dislike.

The overseer, whatever might have been his deficiencies, was a shrewd clear-headed man, and in ferretting out a mystery, had few equals. In the present instance, his wits were sharpened by a sense of duty toward the dead widow, and a desire for revenge. He worked with sagacity, and allowed no incident to escape him, small or large. As might be expected, he soon discovered enough to make his surmises a positive belief.

Many of what the people would have called trifles, were noted down by this man; and the sum of these trifles presented an array dangerous enough to warrant the suspicions even of the most incredulous. The strange appearance of Mrs. Conway's body was remembered—how the bed was all disordered, as if from a violent struggle—the livid spots upon her neck—the open window—and the tracks of some person's feet from the grounds without, through the room—even the fact that Margaret's couch had the next morning borne no sign of occupancy the preceding night—were hunted out by the indefatigable observer. Many other minor and corroborating incidents were also brought to light—the whole making the case of the suspected woman a dark one indeed.

Mr. Phillips applied to the proper authorities for a warrant, and had Margaret lodged in prison, as one who, at the very least, was involved in deep clouds of suspicion.

In the meantime, I myself was as one petrified. Never in all my life did I receive such a shock, as when authentic information was first brought me of the charge against the creole! I could not join the overseer in efforts to worm out the facts of the case; neither could I do aught to screen the murderess of one whom I had so loved. I shut myself up in my room for several days, waiting the conclusion of all these horrible circumstances.

Let me hasten toward that conclusion. I have already dwelt long enough, and too long, on this part of my history, which, notwithstanding the space I have given it, did not occupy more than five or six weeks from the commencement of my acquaintance with Bourne. And I feel glad that I have arrived at the end of the chapter, for my mind revolts at the ideas the narration of these things has already called up in the most disagreeable distinctness.

The overseer continued his investigations, but he might as well have spared himself the trouble. From some train of motives which the great Heart-Viewer alone can fathom, the creole soon after sent for Phillips and myself, and made a full confession. Upon her story as she told it me, and her own acknowledgment, I have given many of the incidents in the preceding two chapters, which, at the time they took place, were totally unknown to me. That very night she committed suicide in her cell. I never saw her again.

# XXIII

*What can mar the sweetest peace?*
*Alcohol!*

TEMPERANCE SONG

THINKING over what had taken place, as I prepared for my journey back to New York, I sometimes fancied that I had been in a dream. The events were so strange—and my own conduct, in respect to some of them, so very unreasonable—that I could hardly bring myself to acknowledge their reality.

Bourne was loth to part with me. Our short friendship had been in many ways very pleasant to us both. It was seldom, indeed, that his retirement was enlivened with the voice of a stranger, or his lonesome hours made glad by the company of one he loved. At the last interview but one which we had before my departure, we discussed in soberness the transactions of the past month. I think that both of us, though we did not so express ourselves at the time, arrived at the conclusion that the drinking-bout, where I and he settled the wretched step of marriage between myself and the creole, was the starting point of all the late evils.

I had hardly arrived in the city, and was at my home there, before a messenger came with a request that I would visit Mr. Lee, my old antiquary friend, who lay very ill. I went, and found him quite as sick as was reported. He knew me at once, however, and rose in his bed to give me a cordial shake of the hand.

"The reason I have sent for you," said he, "is to prepare you for an evidence that, notwithstanding what has passed between us in days gone by, I have thought proper to bestow upon you a portion of that wealth, which it has been my honest pride to gain."

I was amazed with wonder.

"Sir," said I, "what reason can you have for such favor toward one who is to you almost a stranger?"

"My own fancy, Evans," he answered, "my own whim, perhaps. But we are not strangers. And I have always taken blame to myself, that I did not watch over you with a more fatherly care, when you were first thrown, as it were by the hand of Providence, under my charge."

"Indeed, sir," said I, agitated and affected almost to tears, by the old man's kindness, "I did not expect this."

"No matter," said he, "I have made inquiries from time to time about you, though you knew it not, and have kept the track of your course of life. I feel assured that your wild days are over—that experience has taught you wisdom, and that the means I shall place at your command will not be put to improper uses."

The sick merchant, raised himself, and propped against his pillow, enjoined me to listen a few minutes, and he would briefly relate the story of his life—and why it was that in his old age, he was alone in the world, without family or intimates. I shall give his story in my own words.

Stephen Lee, at an early age, received from his father a sufficient capital to enable him to start himself in business, in the mercantile profession. Though he was ambitious, he was prudent, and soon sailed on the forward and brilliant track to success. Fascinated by the charms and accomplishments of a young female cousin, he paid his addresses to her, and they were shortly married.

For several months happiness seemed hovering over them, and all prospects were fair for a life of cloudless content. A year elapsed, and Lee's wife bore him a son. The delighted father now thought that the measure of his joy was full. A few days after her confinement, there began to be a strange lassitude about the young merchant's wife—her health was as good as is ordinary in such cases, but, as the time passed, her countenance grew more pallid and sickly and her eyes lost their lustre. The physician could give no satisfactory account of all this; and Lee himself for some time was in the dark also. But too soon did the fatal truth come to his knowledge, that *ardent spirits* was the cause of that pallor and that lassitude. His wife was an habitual gin-drinker!

Lee, though shocked at this disgusting fact, imagined at first, that the habit had been formed by using drink as a stimulus to keep up her powers of body in her sickness. But it was not so. During the time that had intervened between their marriage, the miserable woman, for very shame, had desisted from the practice. But a single taste, revived the old appetite in all its strength.

It happened one day, when the infant was some ten weeks old, that the mother, stupefied by excess of liquor, let her babe fall against some projecting article of furniture, and [it] received a blow from which it never recovered. In the course of the week the child died, and though the physician never stated the exact cause of its death, it was well understood that the fall from the arms of its drunken mother had been that cause.

Two or three years passed on. Another infant was born to Lee—but it met with a fate not much better than the first. Its death came from neglect and ill nursing.

And the mother—the lovely and educated wife, with whom the merchant had expected to see so much happiness, she was a drunkard. She lingered not long, however, to bear witness to her own and her husband's shame. She sank into the grave, the victim of intemperance.

It was many years before Lee recovered his former tone of character. Naturally cheerful, however, he could not long remain that gloomy being which his misfortunes had for a time made him. He was fond of sporting, and loved the country, which he frequently visited. He loved, too, the old traditions, and reminiscences of the earlier part of our American history, to which he gave up a considerable portion of his leisure. Thus, and in the affairs of his trade, which he still kept on, he had made life pass as evenly and pleasantly as he could.

"You say you are a stranger," he said to me, before I left him, "but you are not half so much so as the rest of the world. My nearest relatives, who were never friendly to me in life, have long since been laid in the grave; and I can make no better disposition of my profits than to give them to one whom [who] I feel confident will not be unwilling to use some part thereof, for suppressing the fearful fiend Intemperance, that has brought such wo upon us both!"

I mused, as I left the place, upon the singular notion of the old man, in remembering me thus. Of course, it was anything but unpleasant to me that I should inherit a respectable competency; and yet I could not help wondering at the method of it.

Not many days elapsed before Lee died, and was laid away to his repose. His will, though the theme of much grumbling to some far-distant connexions, could not be gainsayed, and I came into possession of the property left me.

# XXIV

*The temperance flag! the temperance flag!*
*It is the banner of the free!*
*The temperance flag! the temperance flag!*
*An emblem of our liberty!*

WASHINGTONIAN MINSTREL

So, at an age which was hardly upon the middle verge of life, I found myself possessed of a comfortable property; and, as the term is, [an] "unincumbered" person—which means that I had no wife to love me—no children to please me, and be the recipients of my own affection, and no domestic hearth around which we might gather, as the center of joy and delight. My constitution, notwithstanding the heavy draughts made upon its powers by my habits of intemperance, might yet last me the appointed term of years, and without more than a moderate quantity of the physical ills that man is heir to.

The Marchions were still my firm friends. I visited them often.

"I think, Mr. Evans," said Mrs. Marchion to me one day, "that there is still one thing for you to do, in connection with what has already been your movement upon Temperance. Lately, I find, there is more progress made than we are aware of. People now are not content to abstain merely from the stronger kinds of drinks, but they disuse *all.* I have been reflecting in my own mind upon the subject, and I came to the conclusion that *total* abstinence is indeed the only safe course."

I too had been reflecting in my mind upon the same thing, and I had arrived pretty nearly at the same conclusion.

"My dear madam," said I, "there is more truth in your words, perhaps, than even you yourself imagine. I have tried the old pledge, and I can conscientiously say that I have adhered to it, ever since the day of my signing it; yet, if I were to tell you all the horrors that have been transacted since that time, in reference to my own life, and which I can trace directly to *wine-drinking,* you would be appalled with fear! Total abstinence is indeed the only safe course, and I will put the principle in effect this very evening."

My deeds were as good as my word. Before the sun rose again I had signed the bond—the holy charter with myself, which has never yet been broken; and which, under the blessing of Providence, shall remain inviolate while I continue among the living.

I do not intend to relate the occurrences of my after life. Indeed, were I so disposed, it would be impossible; for I have brought the chain of events down almost to the very day when the reader will be perusing my story. True, several years have passed since my Virginia visit, which resulted so disastrously to some of those with whom I was brought in contact; but the tenor of action has flowed on so smoothly since then, that I have little to tell which would be interesting.

There is one person, however, who has figured in these pages, on whom I would bestow a paragraph before I close. I allude to my old friend, Colby.

As I was passing one day along a street on the eastern side of the city, my course was impeded by [a] crowd, gathered around a tipsy loafer, who was cutting up his antics in the street. The miserable man, it seemed, had been promised by some idle boys enough money to purchase a drink of gin, if he would dance for their amusement. And there he was, going through his disgusting capers.

Pausing a moment, and looking in the man's face, I thought I recollected the features. A second and a third glance convinced me. It was Colby, my early intimate, the tempter who had led me aside from the paths of soberness.

Wretched creature! Had I even wished for some punishment upon his head, in requital of the harm he had done me, a sight of the kind I saw there, would have dissolved all my anger. His apparel looked as though it had been picked up in some mud hole; it was torn in strips and all over soiled. His face was bloated, and his eyes red and swollen. I thought of the morning when I awoke upon the dock, after my long fit of intemperance: the person before me was even more an object of pity than myself on that occasion. His beard had not seen the razor for weeks, and he was quite without shoes.

The spectators laughed, and the heedless children clapped their hands in glee—little thinking of the desecration such a spectacle brought upon the common nature all shared. I felt sick at heart, and hurried away from the place. How had it happened, that I myself did not meet with the same degraded fortune? Was it not indeed miraculous that I—instead of being a counterpart of the poor sot whom I had just been witnessing with feelings I shall not attempt to describe—was occupying a respectable station in society, and on the fair road to a remainder of my life passed in honor and comfort? I blessed my Maker as I thought of these things, and besought His favor on that holy Cause of Reformation, where I had myself cast anchor, and where thousands besides were moored, safe from the wild storm, and from the boiling waves that so threatened to ingulf them.

As it is the usage of story-tellers to give some passing notice of all who have figured in their pages, before those pages are brought to a close, I will here follow the custom; though the small number of such persons, apart from the I, who have been the hero of the tale, will render the task an easy one.

My country relations were not forgotten by me in my good fortune. The worthy uncle, who had kindly housed and fed me when I was quite too small to make him any repayment for that service, received in his old age the means to render his life more easy and happy. My cousins too, had no reason to be sorry for the good-will which they had ever shown toward me. I was never the person to forget a friend, or leave unrequited a favor, when I had the payment of it in my power.

The tavern-keeper, to whom the reader was introduced in the first chapter of my story, dragged out a life of intemperance, a discredit to his family and with little comfort to himself. He was found dead, one winter morning, in a room where in a fit of passion the preceding night he had gone, from that which he usually occupied with his wife. An overturned bottle of brandy was at his side. After his death, the tavern was closed.

My friend, the driver of the market-wagon, became by chance an attendant at some meetings of the temperance advocates. He was a sensible fellow, and listened with open ears to their arguments. In a visit I lately paid to the island of my birth, I found him a whole-hearted and most ardent Washingtonian.

Demaine, I have never been able to light upon more than once or twice, and therefore cannot fully say, what are his fortunes. Probably, however, he is to be numbered among those hundreds of men in our city whose god is fashion and dress; and who, when they are out of sight of their "genteel" acquaintances, have to practice the most miserable economy to "keep up appearances," in the ball-room or the public promenade. Such fellows are as far removed from true gentlemen, as the gilded sun, in stage melo-dramas, from the genuine source of light himself.

The Marchions continued to prosper, as their kindness of heart and their honorable benevolence to the needy, deserved. They are among the most respectable and respected families in the city.

I hear now and then from Bourne. Things are going on in the old way. Phillips has left him, and bought a plantation of his own.

Andrews, my old master, died of grief at the failure of some stock-jobbing operations, wherein a cunning fellow-broker overreached him. His immense possessions, after his death, were found to be as fallacious as the basis on which they had been reared.

The landlord by whom I was so swindled in the country village, after my poor Mary's death, was caught at last in one of his tricks; and not having been as cautious as with me, he now has to repent his wickedness within the walls of the county jail. I hope he will be taught better, by the time that he is at large again.

I have never heard anything further of the Picaroon, or either of his two companions. Undoubtedly, they reached the confines of Sing-Sing before long, after I had the honor of their acquaintance.

Boarding-houses are no more patronized by me. The distaste I formed for them in my memorable search for quarters, when I first came to New York, was never entirely done away with. The comforts of a home are to be had in very few of these places; and I have often thought that the cheerless method of their accommodations drives many a young man to the bar-room, or to some other place of public resort, whence the road to habits of intoxication is but too easy. Indeed, the thought has long been entertained by me, that this matter is not sufficiently appreciated. I would advise every young man to marry as soon as possible, and have a home of his own.

Reader! I have brought my narrative quite to an end. I may be presumptuous to flatter myself that it has been of much amusement to you, though I have had that partly in view. Partly—but not wholly. For I have desired, amid the path we have travelled together, and which is now at an end—that a few seeds of wholesome instruction might be dropped at the same time that we gathered the fruits and the flowers.

# XXV

## CONCLUSION

As works of fiction have often been made the vehicle of morality, I have adopted the novel experiment of making one of the sort a messenger of the cause of Temperance. And though I know not what the decision of the reader may be, I am too strongly armed in the honesty of my intentions, to suppose that there can be any doubt as to the propriety of the *moral* intended to be conveyed—or to fear any attack upon the story, as regards its principles.

To expatiate upon the ruins and curses which follow the habitual use of strong drink, were at this time almost a stale homily. A great revolution has come to pass within the last eight or ten years. The dominion of the Liquor Fiend has been assaulted and battered. Good men and strong have come up to the work of attack. Warriors, with large hands, and with girded loins, are waiting with resolution, and their energies are devoted to the battle. They are taking the place of those who are wearied, and in their turn give way to others, who have new and greater strength. Will the old fortress yield? It *must,* sooner or later. It may be compared to some ivy-crowned castle, some strong tower of the olden time, with its flanked battlements, and its guards pacing on the top of its walls, and laughing to scorn all the devices of those who came against it. The red banner floated on its topmost height—inscribed with its fearful watchword, "Disgrace and Death!" And a million victims came every year, and yielded themselves to their ruin under its control. But the foes of the Castle of Orgies stepped forth in array, and swore to one another that they would devote their lives to the work of reform. Long did that haughty structure resist every blow—firmly did it defy every besieger. But the might of a good motive is more than the highest strength of wickedness; and at last the bars of the gates began to give way, and the thick walls cracked. An outpost was driven in, and a tower fell. How tremendous the shout then that arose from the men who were fighting the good fight, and the faces of their antagonists paled with fear! So they kept on. And other parts of the foundation were undermined, and the heavy stanchions were burst asunder, and the forces of the Red Fiend have been routed, band after band, until but a little are left; and they will soon have to retreat, and go the way of their brethren.

The good of the present age are smiling upon the cause of Temperance. It is indeed a holy cause. How many widows' tears it has assuaged—and how many poor wretched men it has taken by the hand, and led to reputation and comfort once more. It seems to me, that he who would speak of the efforts of the Temperance Societies with a sneer, is possessed of a very heedless and bigoted, or a very wicked disposition. It is true, that the dictates of a classic and most refined taste, are not always observed by these people; and the fashionable fop, the exquisite, or the pink of what is termed "quality," might feel not at home among them. But to persons with clear heads, and with breasts where philanthropy and a desire for the good of their fellows have a resting-place, I am fully content to leave the decision whether, after all, there be not a good deal of *intellectuality* engaged in the Temperance movement.

The Reformers have one great advantage, too, which makes up for any want of polish, or grace. They are sincere, and speak with the convictions of their own experience. In all ages, a revolution for the better, when started, has found its advocates among the poorer classes of men. From them, it gradually rises, until it pervades all ranks of society. It has happened so in this case. The few men who met together in Baltimore, and formed a compact with themselves to abstain from those practices which had been so injurious to them, little thought how their principles were to spread, and how they would be pointed back to with admiration, from the rich as well as the poor—the learned as well as the ignorant.

They called themselves WASHINGTONIANS. Long may the name be honored—and long may it continue to number among those who are proud to style themselves by the title—upright and noble spirits, determined never to turn back from the work, or to discredit the name they bear, and the Society to which they belong!

Any one who has attended the meetings of the temperance people, cannot but be amazed and delighted at the enthusiasm which pervades them. It is not confined to one sex, or to any particular age or class. It spreads over all. Men and women join in it. Young people, even boys and girls, are inoculated with the fervor, and are heard about the streets, singing the temperance songs, and conversing upon the principles of the doctrine, by which their fathers or brothers have been regenerated and made happy. The enthusiasm I mention, has not been limited, either, to one City or one State. It is felt over every part of this Republic, and accounts come to us of the wondrous doings of Temperance in Maine, while the same hour, in the Western mail, we receive the story of how many new converts there are in Illinois. Perhaps on no occasion has there been a spectacle so full of moral splendor. A whole nation forsaking an evil mania, which has hitherto made it the mark of scorn to those who, coming from abroad, have noticed this one foul blot in contradistinction to all the other national good qualities—and turning a goodly portion of its mighty powers to the business of preventing others from forming the same habits; and redeem [redeeming], as far as practicable, those who have already formed them: I consider it a sight which we may properly call on the whole world to admire!

In the story which has been narrated in the preceding pages, there is given but a faint idea of the dangers which surround our young men in this great city. On all sides, and at every step, some temptation assails them; but all the others joined together, are nothing compared with the seductive enchantments which have been thrown around the practice of intoxication, in some five or six of the more public and noted taverns called "musical saloons," or some other name which is used to hide their hideous nature. These places are multiplying. The persons engaged in the sale of ardent spirits are brought to see that their trade, unless they can join something to it, as a make-weight, will shortly vanish into thin air, and their gains along with it. Thus they have hit upon the expedient of MUSIC, as a lure to induce customers, and in too many cases with fatally extensive success.

I would warn that youth whose eye may scan over these lines, with a voice which speaks to him, not from idle fear, but the sad knowledge of experience, how bitter are the consequences attending, these musical drinking-shops. They are the fit portals of ruin and inevitably lead thither. I have known more than one young man, whose prospects for the future were good—in whom hope was strong, and energy not wanting—but all poisoned by these pestilent places, where the mind and the body are both rendered effeminate together.

To conclude, I would remark that, if my story meets with that favor which writers are perhaps too fond of relying upon, my readers may hear from me again, in the [a] method similar to that which has already made us acquainted.

THE AUTHOR.